# A Seeker's Harvest

A Life and Legacy with ALS

*[signature: Kevin Pollari]*

As told by **KEVIN POLLARI**
Written by Heidi Schauer

*Tim,*
*May there be something in Kevin's journey (and my first book project) that is special for the journey you are on.*
*— Heidi*

A Seeker's Harvest
Copyright © 2015 by Kevin Pollari and Heidi Schauer

FIRST EDITION DECEMBER 2015

Edited by Kelly Paradis. Designed by Andrea McArdle and Heidi Schauer. Front cover painting and photography by Jessie DeCorsey.

The information in this book is being used as an education tool to share with you the details of Kevin Pollari's life journey. This information is not medical advice. For health, well-being and possible side effects it is advised that you consult a health professional.

All rights reserved, including the rights to reproduce this book or portions thereof in any form whatsoever.

ISBN-13: 978-1502827012
ISBN-10: 1502827018

This book is dedicated by Kevin Pollari:
To all who find themselves with a terminal or chronic condition.
I hope this will help give you hope and perspective as to how our food and thoughts affect every cell in our bodies.

And by Heidi Schauer:
To my beloved husband and beautiful children,
best friends, teachers and family.
For a bird cannot fly without wind beneath its wings.

# A Seeker's Harvest

A Life and Legacy with ALS

As told by **Kevin Pollari**
Written by Heidi Schauer

"If I could give you a piece of advice, I would encourage you to be a seeker for what works for *you*. Be someone who doesn't simply accept what you are told. Be someone who doesn't leave their health solely in the hands of mainstream doctors or other people. Doctors and other people, my friends, are human beings. Human beings are imperfect. If something isn't working for you, search for something that hasn't been found yet. Turn over every rock, trudge down every trail, comb over the details, and be a seeker. Do what you can to be in charge of this life that you have to live."

– Kevin Pollari

# INTRODUCTION
## Heidi Schauer

The story you are about to read has come to life through great sacrifice, an abundance of passion, and a deep desire to authentically share the life and ALS (amyotrophic lateral sclerosis) experiences of Kevin Pollari. ALS, or Lou Gehrig's disease, is a motor neuron disease known only to be fatal. The hope is that you, the reader, through the words on these pages, gain insight into the world of ALS and learn something of value for the journey you are on – whatever that journey may be. The result of a two year project, this book has been an educational adventure and spiritual awakening.

My journey with Kevin Pollari and Leslie Hitchcock began August 15, 2013, outside Flaherty's Arden Bowl in Arden Hills, Minnesota. I was hosting the second annual Jim Cunningham Fishes and Loaves Food & School Supply Drive in honor of what would have been my father's 57th birthday. Kevin and Leslie came that evening with canned goods and stories about familial ALS research, stem cell treatments, benefits of coconut oil, and a discovery of "leaky gut" and eating Beyond Organic. I was impressed. Hoping to get to the bottom of extreme allergy intolerances I asked questions and took notes. Long after the sun set, I was still trying to learn all I could about possible solutions to my struggles. As the evening was coming to an end, Kevin said to me, "My friends tell me I should write a book." And that was all it took. Telling such a thing to a woman who believes in dreaming BIG always has consequences. A seed was planted.

"Plunge boldly into the thick of life, and seize it where you will, it is always interesting." -- Johann Wolfgang von Goethe,

German writer and statesman.

August 21, 2013, neither of us knowing what would actually be required of us to successfully co-create a book, Kevin Pollari and I began storytelling, writing and composing for *A Seeker's Harvest*. The experience is one that has changed my life and given to me unexpected perspectives and a new depth to my faith. Kevin's desire to find the root cause of his ALS symptoms, and his drive and persistence to do what he can to slow his ALS progression, is admirable. He has taught me to never stop seeking, never stop learning, and never take my health or capabilities for granted. He has shown me the importance of being greatly brave in loving others and myself. He has reminded me of the value of service, and the importance of communication and expressing sincere gratitude. And he has given me a friendship and an experience I will cherish always doing what I can to be fully aware of the great honor it is to witness the life of others.

This is Kevin's story.

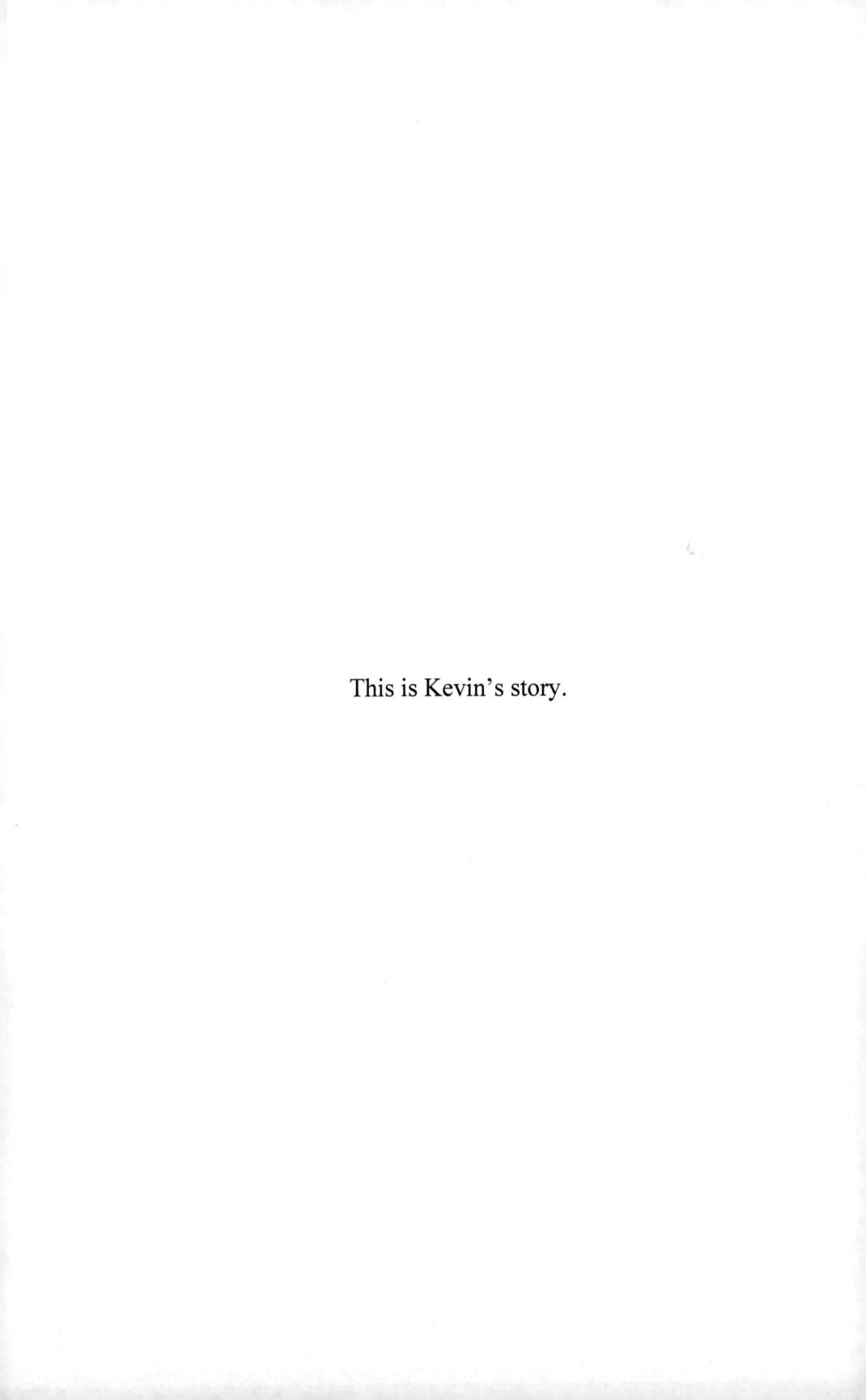

**October 1, 2014 | 39 months after diagnosis**

    I was taking an afternoon nap, and Leslie, my fiancé, left a little before 5 o'clock p.m. while I was sleeping. She was anxious to go kayaking with a friend on a nice day. Bertha, my caregiver, had always shown up at five so Leslie felt comfortable leaving. I woke up from my nap and waited, in bed, watching the clock: 5:05, 5:10, 5:15, 5:30. I was alone.

    Anxiety started to set in. What if the power goes out right now? What if the house caught fire? What if I have to go to the bathroom? Is Bertha okay? Has she been in a car accident? I decided I couldn't do anything so I better just relax. I continued to stare at the clock, 5:45, 6:00, 6:15, all the way up to 6:40.

    Luckily, I had texted my sister Lynn earlier in the day that it would be great to see her if she had time and could drop in. She stopped by, saw the house lights all out with the van in the driveway. She was smart enough to come in and ask, "Are you in here?" Then she discovered me.

    Was I upset? Damn sure. I'm so dependent.

-Kevin Pollari

# Seeds of Change
### 2014 | 39 months after diagnosis

By October 2014, I was having this realization of the burden; this realization of quality of life. My friend Steve, he's an ALS guy, his lung capacity was at 86/87 percent. He'll be around a long time, but his quality of life — quality of life is something you have to consider.

This past summer was hard on me. Not that I haven't been having fun, it's just – I wanted to go swimming. I wanted to go boating. I wanted to go four wheeling. I really miss that stuff. Yeah, friends say they will take me out and I can do these things, but it's not the same. It's not the same as ripping off my own t-shirt, running through the hot sand as fast as I can into the cool Minnesota lake water. I practically grew up on Snail Lake in Shoreview. Summer days, hot or not, I rode my bicycle there and spent hours holding my breath, diving under water and exploring.

In my teenage years, if I had access to a boat on any particular day, I used my aqua plane, a self-made toy that looked like a cross with foot pegs and fins, which we towed behind a boat at trolling speed. When I was the operator of the aqua plane, I would put on my goggles, lay stomach-side down, pull myself onto it and prepare for an adventurous ride. While the boat pulled me around, I pushed the hand flaps up and dived down into the water for what seemed like a thousand feet without using any energy. Or, what was even more fun was to push one flap up and one flap down and spin around under the water. The aqua plane was the best. It's one of my childhood summers great memories. But I suppose for this story, because it is somewhat important to know who I am and where I come from, we should start from the beginning. So let's go back a moment to before I was born.

# Those Who Came Before Me
## 1800s-1940s

My father's family is Finnish and they are known for their Sisu, a reference to stoic determination, bravery, and perseverance. My great grandfather immigrated with his family in the 1890s. He served the upper Midwest as a Lutheran preacher until he suffered a fatal heart attack. My grandfather, Charlie, was a well builder. He met his wife Aune Hill in Ironwood, Michigan. They raised one son, my dad Charlie, in Maple, Wisconsin. My grandfather operated the family well building business until he died at a young age from a heart attack. Being an only child, my dad connected with his many cousins and he was delighted to raise a family with 6 kids. We recently learned that my Grandma Aune's family were actually Vikings from the Orkney Islands who settled in Finland somewhere around the 12th century. So, I am proud to say I am a true Viking. But, it is now known that the Viking genes may have founded the genetic mutations that spawn ALS. There are epidemic studies showing a trail of increased ALS along the Viking exploration routes. (http://alsn.mda.org/article/c90rf72-bound-repeat-itself) It is also interesting that while we know this disease is a genetic mutation within our family in the US, there is no data about the presence of ALS in our family living in Finland.

## To Live in Fear
**1960s**

In 1962, the civil rights movement was in full swing. John F. Kennedy was president of the United States of America while John Glenn had become the first American to orbit the earth. I read somewhere that the Mona Lisa was exhibited for the first time in the United States at the National Gallery of Art in Washington D.C. that year. It was also the year Bob Dylan released his debut album, and the first Target store opened in Roseville, Minnesota. The world was growing and changing and I was eager to be a part of it. So eager, in fact, that I was born March 30, 1962 in the entryway of North Memorial Hospital in Robbinsdale, Minnesota at three a.m. in the middle of a snowstorm.

My parents Dick and Lois Pollari already had three kids by the time I arrived. Brother Keith was fifteen, sister Anne was eleven, and Jan just five when I entered this world. We lived in a three-bedroom rambler on Lilac Lane in Shoreview, not far from an ammunition plant. My mom told me once that she and my dad didn't want to settle right in the city of St. Paul and back in 1954, Shoreview was kind of "out in the country." One day, Mom and Dad were on their way up north to Grandma Aune's when they saw a sign for a new housing development inviting GIs to inquire. That's when the GI bill was enacted and they were giving GIs loans and it was a big deal. When Mom and Dad went to look at the house, there wasn't even a road yet. They parked up on Rice Street and walked down to the gray/blue house with the brick front. It had three bedrooms and a single car garage and Dad was so determined to buy it he told Mom he'd sell the car and walk to work if he had to. They raised our entire family in that house and lived there until just before my dad died.

I spent nineteen years of my life in that rambler not thinking once about what may or may not have drained into the ground or run into the water from that ammunition plant. Now, I think about that sometimes.

I'm told when Lynn was brought home eighteen months after I settled in, I called her doo-doo. To this day we joke about doo-doo. I haven't heard if Lynn or I had any name suggestions for Lora when she joined us two years after Lynn. Dad, Mom, Keith, Anne, Jan, our wiener dog, Schmitty, and my two younger sisters Lynn and Lora – we all liked living on Lilac Lane in our house by the woods.

Childhood years are funny when you think about it – what we remember and what we don't. I'm learning now, one way or another, the memories of our experiences exist. But my memories of my first five years of life are sketchy in my mind. I recall only a few things: Schmitty, my sisters, and feeling afraid. The whole world was afraid back then.

October 14, 1962 chaos broke out after a U-2 flight over Cuba captured photos of Soviet nuclear weapons being installed. The following day the Soviet Union and the United States found themselves in a standoff, and the whole world worried about a nuclear war. No matter how tiny a person is, war and fear make it into the memory bank. People built bomb shelters and stockpiled supplies. Mom and Dad filled our basement with food and emergency gear. They bought Kool-Aid and other additives to put in water so it would be drinkable.

March 1967, my brother Keith traveled to Fort Sill, Oklahoma where he became part of the 8th Battalion, 4th Artillery. That July, the men of the 8th Battalion, 4th Artillery flew to Tacoma, Washington, boarded a troop ship, the USNS UPSHUR, and set sail for Vietnam. On August 12, 1967 they arrived in Da Nang with a mission to support the 1st and 3rd Marine Divisions. It was a mission the Pollari house could feel, even from thousands of miles away.

When Mom wasn't volunteering for the DFL Party, serving such people as Hubert Humphrey, Rosalie Butler, Wendell Anderson and Rudy Perpich, she was at home, smoking Vantage cigarettes and pacing the floor praying there would be no knock on the door. Dad worked nights as a proofreader in St. Paul at West Publishing Co., so us kids would sit with Mom listening to Walter Cronkite while we searched the names scrolling across the bottom of our black and white television set hoping Keith Pollari never appeared. It never did.

Cigarette after cigarette Mom worried about Keith when he was away and even after he returned. She worried about the possibility of nuclear war, too. It had flooded the newspaper and evening news. Everybody was worrying about that. The worry and the cigarettes would cause Mom chest pains some evenings, and in those days people took nitroglycerin for things like chest pains. Mom would take the nitroglycerin and my sisters and I would worry about war, our brother, and our mom.

Keith returned home from Vietnam after an injury. I don't know the details of what he saw or what he did, but I know he was a photographer. In our basement, somewhere down by the supplies, there was a shelf full of slide rings. Each ring had a couple hundred slides. When Keith returned home he went to the basement, got the slide rings full with images he had captured during the war, and burned all of them.

He never told me anything about it, about the war. When I would ask him, he would say, "I lost my innocence." I only knew what it was like here as a small child, with Mom, Dad and the other kids. I wondered why wars needed to happen. Why were people killing each other? Why would I want to grow up if I was just going to be killed? At five years old, I was sure I would grow up and have to go to war, and at that young age I wondered why I would want to grow up at all. I had questions that had no good answers.

To this day Keith's ears ring and he doesn't like fireworks. When the sun goes down on the Fourth of July, while the rest of our family gathers, ooohing and ahhhing at the colors and the patterns and the beauty of Independence Day, Keith goes inside. War takes a toll, even forty years later.

# A Celebration of Independence
## 1960s-1970s | ages 5-15

By the mid-1970s, Mom was working for Governor Perpich's administration. July 4, 1976 marked the 200th anniversary of the adoption of the Declaration of Independence. She was the Director of the 1976 Minnesota Bicentennial Commission and organized celebrations for the whole state.

From the time I was five until I was fifteen, Mom was working during the day and Dad was sleeping after his overnight shift at the printing company. With limited supervision and no reason to stay indoors I spent most of my days outside exploring the grasslands, oak forests, steep hills and the sandpit behind my house. Now it's called Vadnais-Snail Lake Regional Park, but back then it was just our woods. The neighborhood kids had bonfires and deep wood adventures. We built our own zip line, played Kick the Can, Freeze Tag or Mother May I? Sometimes we even invented our own games. We were rarely bored.

The summer of 1967, I had an other world experience. I was 5 years old, and I heard a voice. In those days we were heating the house with fuel oil. On the outside of our home was a pipe with a cap on it. Some caps had locks, some didn't. Ours didn't. I thought it was kind of cool when the guy with the oil tanker would come, so for some reason, on this day, I thought maybe I would pour sand into the pipe where the man pours the oil, and he would come with his truck and his hose and his fuel to see me. I walked over to the pipe, unscrewed the cap, and was getting ready to pour the sand from my hand into the pipe when I heard a big loud voice say, "Kevin!"

I dropped the sand and ran around the corner of the house, looking over my shoulder and all around wondering who said my name. I saw no one. There was no one there. *Who said my name?* I didn't pour sand into that pipe that day or ever. And I didn't forget that feeling that someone was watching me, and they would know if I had done something wrong when I knew better.

June 1968, my brother Keith returned home from Vietnam. I was 6 years old. Keith was twenty-one and preoccupied with processing what he had just experienced during the war. My brother and I spent little time together. He went to work for a furniture company, and though I continued to fear war and death, my childhood was blessed with freedom and the beauty of nature.

There were regular trips to see Grandma Aune in Maple. We kids would sleep upstairs where it smelled like moth balls. I still think of Grandma Aune when I smell moth balls, and I recall the spinning chair, the knick-knacks everywhere, and outside, the yard that ran into the woods.

Lynn, Lora and I would hunt for agates down near the railroad tracks. In those early years one afternoon of searching would successfully fill our pockets, fueling our desire to do it again. Some days we would put pennies or nickels on the tracks and wait for the train to go by and flatten them. We were curious and pleased with simple treasures.

The outdoors was not the only treat in Maple. Grandma Aune was a good cook. I remember her always wearing an apron and a smile, my sisters and I enjoying her homemade deep fried donuts, anise bread and Limppu (Finnish bread). Like our father and his cousins, my siblings and I made many wonderful memories in Maple. But our abundance of joy was accompanied by some sorrow.

December 10, 1970, Grandma Aune stayed late at work. Around 6:30 p.m. she walked out the back door of the school, and while locking the door, slipped and fell on the ice. Hours passed before someone heard her cries for help. Once they found her they brought her to the hospital. Grandma Aune's time had come. At the hospital a blood clot in her leg went into her heart killing her at the age of 62. Of course these days things would be different, but that was 1970. She was healthy, vibrant and still working. Grandma Aune's death was a shock. I was eight years old and remember seeing my dad very sad. I remember, too, the roses. I had never really smelled roses until my grandmother's funeral and every time I've smelled them since, I've thought of her.

For a few years after Grandma Aune passed, our family kept her house, renting it out to various people and staying in the "little house" when we would make the trek from Shoreview to Maple. After we sold the house, my family continued to visit Maple. We would camp at the Brule River campground in a small pop-up camper that my sisters and I still, to this day, can't understand how we all fit in. I have great memories of tubing and canoeing, watching fireflies and squealing with my siblings while we swatted mosquitos. My happiest times were spent outdoors.

In school, I did try some sports. In sixth grade, I took up gymnastics, diving and the pole vault in track. I wanted to be the world's record holder in the pole vault. I didn't have the height and speed to become a world record holder, so I moved on from that dream.

At the age of twelve I became a businessman. I placed a sign in my front yard for a bicycle repair shop. Five bucks an hour. Shortly after that I designed the neighborhood communication system. I had found a big spool of wire under the work bench in the basement, so my friends and I set up wires to go from my house to the house across the street and the house behind me. With a couple of my friends dialed in I could say "meet outside" into a microphone through my stereo and have it come out through their speakers. Since our homes only had single phone lines and most of us had sisters, this means of communication was necessary. And it was fun.

Peter Carlson was my friend who lived directly behind me. There were four boys in that family. He had an older brother, Chris, and a younger brother, Paul, but Pete was my age. There was Brian Patterson and Dave Coats and Art Henningfield. Art's father had a shop, and Art, like me, was mechanical. So we made things like go-karts.

And when we were thirteen, we built a bomb.

There was no ill intent or anything like that, we just wanted to make it go boom. Down the street a contractor was building some homes and there was a garage that wasn't finished yet. A big pile of lumber scraps from the workers sat in the middle of it. We put our little bomb in that pile of scrap, lit the candle, and ran home. It was five or ten minutes before we heard the explosion. Maybe another five or ten before we heard the fire engines coming down the road. Unfortunately, our bomb started the pile of wood on fire. That made quite a neighborhood stir. But the house was okay. Mom and Dad never found out about that, and Art and I never did that again. I did, however, have many other adventures.

A real positive part of my junior high years when I needed someone to look up to was at the YMCA on Lexington Avenue where I met a life guard named Bart. Bart's real name was Ken Allmun, but we all called him Bart. He encouraged me at the diving board, and became my friend. I loved to ski, and in the winter time he would invite me to go skiing with him at Afton Alps where he was a ski patrol. He went to school at Bethel College and ended up working for 3M. We still stay in touch, and I'm still thankful he was generous with his compliments and encouragement and was and is a kind person. You can never have too many kind people in your world.

My mom did, however, help me get my voice heard.

The cross street to Lilac Lane is Hodgson Road, which at that time was gravel on each side and not quite as fast and furious as it is today, but it was still busy. By second grade I was riding my bike down Hodgson to school. A few years later, I put a five horse Briggs and Stratton engine on my Schwinn ten-speed bike and raced cars down Hodgson. One of my horrible Hodgson moments happened in the winter when I was thirteen and a bunch of us were throwing snowballs at cars. It was a March storm and the snow was heavy and deep. We threw a snowball at the wrong car. They were able to stop their car very quickly and start running after us. After realizing I couldn't run as fast as these guys, I dove into a bush. I remember being scared to death with my heart in my throat as the group of guys stood feet away from me saying, "Those kids are gonna get it!"

Thankfully, none of us got caught.

At some point, my adventures on Hodgson and the help of my mother led to a petition to persuade people that we needed shoulders on Hodgson Road. I submitted the petition with a letter to the county to make putting shoulders on Hodgson a priority. I can't say for sure if it was the letter that helped, but maybe it did. The county put shoulders on each side of Hodgson, and to me, it was a big deal. In my mind, my voice had been heard.

Many weekends I was still making the trek to the family farm in Maple with my parents. One of my greatest Maple moments was when I was 15 years old and my mom and dad drove with the pop-up camper so late in the night we parked in Uncle Ted's yard before going on to the campground the next morning. My friend, Lee Selvog, was with us and we slept on Maple Hill that night where we saw the most amazing northern lights. Those lights, Aurora Borealis, happen when particles from the sun enter Earth's atmosphere and collide fiercely with gas atoms. You need specific conditions to see them: solar flares and a dark, clear night. And though we now have devices that can help predict the aurora activity level, the northern lights are still unpredictable. Beautiful, but unpredictable. A lot like the journey of our lives.

# The Great Knife Throw
## 1978 | age 16

Sometimes people get a feeling or a sense that they just know something. That they have been somewhere before or seen someone before or have experienced this exact moment before. Maybe there's a feeling that they shouldn't get into a car with a group of people or they shouldn't go out this particular night. Maybe the hair on their arms stands up. Maybe they feel as if someone is standing directly behind them, a presence, but when they look no one is there. Still, they have a feeling. Often, such feelings are dismissed. Sometimes we look back and see the moment was actually something bigger.

After the mysterious voice I heard call out my name when I was five, the next real moment that sticks out in my mind as "something" is a moment I had as a teenager.

While I enjoyed skiing, swimming and such, I had never thrived at sports in school. But I did have really good hand/eye coordination. I was an excellent juggler and could play an intense game of ping pong. I was more of a "games of skill and chance" kind of guy. Knife throwing fits perfectly into that. This day, this knife throw, was noteworthy.

My friends and I liked to hang out and camp in the Ramsey County open space site between Snail Lake and Hodgson Road. One night, about dusk, we were setting up camp. We had set up our two tents and made a fire, and I was practicing throwing this 8-inch knife just for the fun of throwing it.

My friends, Dave Coates from the neighborhood and Lee Selvog from school, were sitting around the fire when I saw an oak tree with the perfect spot to make a target; about chest height there was this bend. Walking over to it, I carved a two-inch square with my knife. Using the blade, I lifted and peeled off the tree's bark. My intention was to stand back on the other side of the fire pit and throw the knife in such a way it would stick right in the middle of the two-inch target that I made. No practice tries, just throw it. In my mind I thought *for this knife to end up in the mark on that tree, it will have to spin four-and-a-half times.* As I walked to my spot, I thought about the four-and-a-half spins and envisioned the knife already stuck dead center in the small mark on the tree.

Dave and Lee were laughing around the fire unaware of what I was doing. I stood back, felt this rush of energy surge through me, yelled, "Watch this!" pulled my hand back and cast my arm forward releasing the knife. Before it landed I knew in my mind right where the blade was going to lodge itself into the tree trunk. I know that sounds unbelievable, but it wasn't one of those "Oh, I hope it lands there" or "Hey, who knows?" It was a vivid picture in my mind and this feeling that the moment I released the knife it was in that tree, dead center on the mark I made.

The knife circled through the air exactly four-and-a-half times and BAM! Thirty feet from where I was standing, in the middle of the mark I had made on the tree, was the knife. In the exact spot I envisioned it.

You may be thinking "So what?" or "Lucky!" But this was a moment. This was a feat for any expert knife thrower, and it created this feeling I had not experienced before. It was just crazy. And as crazy as it may sound, I felt that the experience of seeing in my mind exactly where that knife was going to land was something bigger. Spirit assisted. God assisted. I felt seeing where the knife was before the knife was actually there, and feeling what I felt, meant something.

I had not been a child who spent a great number of days in church. Growing up I wouldn't say my parents were particularly religious people. I also wouldn't say they weren't. Sometimes on Sundays they would load us kids into the car and drop us off at the church up the street on Chippewa. Church wasn't denounced in our home, but we weren't sitting around the dinner table saying prayers and giving thanks; we weren't getting ready for bedtime by kneeling and folding our hands.

The idea of religion, for me, didn't become of great importance until I grew up and got married. But on the day of this great knife throw, I felt something. I told my friends, Dave and Lee, and the whole thing didn't seem to mean anything to them. They giggled and laughed and made fun of my feelings of this being a magical moment.

Did I really know the knife was going to land exactly where I pictured it in the tree? I think so. The same way I knew my dreams had at times become reality and I could predict certain futures based on certain dreams.

# Gotta Have the Green
### 1978-79 | age 16-17

At sixteen, my biggest dreams made working to earn my own money a priority. My summer days were spent putting in long hours and saving whatever dollars I could. I was a real quick study so my brother Keith hired me to help in the custom cabinet shop he owned and operated. He had a contract with an architect that had a lot of really big million dollar homes. Each summer, all the way through college, I worked there part-time and learned the craft of cabinetry.

The summer of 1978, when I had earned enough, I bought a 1971 royal blue Chevy pickup truck that had a spotlight and a wooden topper. With the remaining $3,000 I had saved, I put a down payment on a duplex at 563 Western Avenue in Frogtown, a neighborhood in St. Paul. To be in high school and own my own house, which I was going to rent out for additional income, was a big deal. It was something that set me apart from other kids my age. Working was going to get me out of high school. At least for a few hours.

During my junior and senior years at Mounds View High School, there was a work program offered. By senior year I wanted to be anywhere but school, so I signed up for the work program. While I had always been fairly smart and did just fine in school, I had little to no desire to sit there. Bleh! Each day while other kids were in class, I went to work for Michael Lipshults at Plants Inc., a large wholesale plant company in Roseville.

Mostly I helped Michael unload truckloads of plants and later load plant materials into customer's cars. It was easy work and it got me outside and moving around instead of inside sitting at a desk. And I was still learning stuff.

One day, while Michael and I were working, we were talking about this big garden Michael had at his lake place in Wisconsin.

"It's maintenance-free, no weeds," he said.

"No weeds? How?" I asked.

"I use pieces of shag carpeting."

"Shag carpeting?"

That was a new one. I had never heard of someone using shag carpeting in his garden before.

At sixteen, I didn't give the carpeting much thought. But in my forties, learning about my body and the importance of what I was consuming, Michael Lipshultz and his shag carpet garden popped into my head. Reflecting on that conversation, I realized no matter how nice it may have been at the time for Michael to have no weeds, the convenience of using shag carpeting may have come with a health cost. Michael died in his thirties from brain cancer. I'm not saying his shag carpet garden caused his brain cancer. But it certainly didn't do anything to help not cause it. That whole "you are what you eat" saying has merit. The food we consume is part of the plants we grow which is part of the soil we put the plant seed into. Whatever is in the soil is in the plant which is in the food. This is why pesticides and herbicides are such a big deal. This is why people are protesting Monsanto. This, in part, is possibly why Michael, who was eating foods and plants grown in, around and between shag carpeting particles, did not live beyond his thirties.

But back to senior year, what was great about working with Michael at Plants, Inc. during the school year was I spent some of my work time working there, and sometimes, Michael would give me the freedom to go work on the duplex that I owned.

Being a landlord at the age of sixteen is anything but easy. Many of my tenants, because I was "a kid," did not take me seriously and that made collecting rent a challenge. Good thing I've never been one to give up just because something is challenging.

By my eighteenth birthday I declared I would be a millionaire by the time I turned thirty. It was an ambitious goal I planned to achieve.

## Girls, Girls, Girls
**1980 | age 18**

Kathy Luken was at my 18th birthday party. She was the only real girlfriend I had in high school. I had lots of girlfriends in elementary school, but in junior high and high school? Not so much. My senior year my mom said "Maybe it's time to find a girlfriend." So I did.

Kathy and I hung out, went to the high school football games and went to prom. Prom was in St. Paul that year. We rented a hotel room. We drank sloe gin. Kathy got sick. We crashed for the night.

After graduating high school, Kathy and I went on a seven-day trip to the Big Horn Mountains in Wyoming to go back packing. It was early September. We parked, signed in at a little ranger's station not talking to anyone, grabbed our gear and started up the mountain. The weather looked fine. But three days into our trip, at a higher elevation, a snowstorm hit. We had spent the previous days hiking. That third day, we had just finished climbing Cloud Peak, a really high peak in the area. The heavy, wet snow collapsed our tent at four in the morning, soaking everything. At daybreak we had to make our way out of there. Everything soaked, it weighed much more than it did on the way up, and the trails were covered with snow. Luckily, I was good with quadrangle maps, and back then I was able to walk all day long. We started hiking back down the mountains at 6 a.m., but it wasn't easy. By mid-morning Kathy was struggling.

"I can't go any further," she said.

"You have to," I said, "You have to go further or we're going to die right here."

We walked and walked, a good seven miles through snow, up and down the mountain. I will never forget the feeling of coming over the last little hill and seeing my blue truck. *We're going to make it!* I thought. *We're actually going to make it.*

We made it to the truck, soaked, exhausted and with no truck keys. In the process of surviving the snowstorm, I somehow lost the keys. Thankfully, I had a second set in a little magnetic box under the front wheel well. So Kathy and I loaded our gear into the truck and we drove it to a tiny town to a little motel where we were able to dry off and warm up a bit. Then we drove up to Devils Tower National Monument. And as luck would have it, somewhere on the trail I lost my second set of truck keys. So, I pulled out the ignition switch and played with some wires. At the ranger's station, I left my name and address and a note asking if anyone finds any keys, please send them, and we started heading home.

A month after we returned from the Big Horn Mountains, Kathy left to live in France for a year. There were no cell phones back then and we hadn't discussed any, "Hey, I'm waiting for you," so shortly after Kathy left, I assumed our relationship was over. When she returned a year later and came to visit me, she found me laying on my bed (fully clothed) with a new girlfriend. She grabbed a champagne glass from the dresser, threw it at me, and stormed out of the room. The glass busted right above my head, and while I thought that was kind of humorous, I wasn't laughing when my new girlfriend walked out too. Kathy had given me confidence that I was attractive and capable of navigating unexpected situations. Maybe she gave me a little too much confidence.

In spring of 1981, I started school at the University of Minnesota. I still didn't love school, but I took some drafting courses, some architecture and some marketing. I was working construction full-time, taking classes part-time and just checking to see what else I might want to study. I also started a poster framing company.

It was an easy way to make money. I ordered posters and framed them in my living room. At the time, my parents owned a fourplex on Grand Avenue, in the area of the Grand Old Days parade. I launched my business during Grand Old Days and kept pretty busy with people interested in framed posters. My favorite job was custom Lautrec posters for a bar.

Shortly after I began my framing business, my parents bought a small green four bedroom house close to the University of Minnesota. It had a brick fireplace and a spiral staircase that went up into a loft. My friends and I were able to live there. I lived up in the loft. In the front yard I displayed a steel sculpture I made that would clang in the wind. It was kind of cool. I wish I had a picture of it. That house had some epic parties. What I loved most about it was that it introduced me to my friend John Roche, the neighbor across the street who owned a BMW motorcycle.

He'd be out polishing his motorcycle all the time. I said hi to him a couple times and he never really responded. Then one day I said, "Well, then don't say hi."

"Oh, hi!" he hollered back. And that was the beginning of our friendship.

John had short hair, was in the Navy and a very fit marathon runner. He would call at eight o'clock Saturday morning and say, "Kev, seize the day! I just ran ten miles. What are you doing?" What I was not doing was running ten miles before 8 a.m.

One day John took me with him to a job site in Eden Prairie where his brother Phil was building some townhomes. John introduced me to him. Phil and I, both construction guys, started talking and eventually working together. We, too, became friends, and to this day Phil is one of my best, like-minded friends.

# The Grateful Dead
### 1982 | age 20

What is life without friendship and music? For a short while, I followed the Grateful Dead with some friends. On August 3, 1982, I was in the Starlight Theater in Kansas City, Missouri. It was a small venue and the security was so preoccupied with keeping people contained I was able to walk right up to the front and put my elbows on stage about six feet away from Jerry Garcia. There I was mid-concert listening to the music and watching the man himself. It was a beautiful evening.

After that show, my buddies and I got in the car. Since I was the most sober, I drove. Just out of town one of the guys had to go to the bathroom – isn't that how it always goes? He insisted on pulling into this abandoned gas station.

"Not a good idea," I argued.

"Come on, just pull around back," he said.

I pulled into the parking lot and started to go around back when two squad cars squealed in after us, their lights on, sirens blaring. They collected all of our driver's licenses. Then they went back and got into their car. We're all thinking, *Oh, boy, we're screwed*. And a couple minutes later they must have gotten a call or something, because they rolled their windows down, threw out our driver's licenses, and peeled out of the parking lot. Yes! We gladly picked up our belongings and headed to Red Rocks for another show.

Seeing the Grateful Dead at the Alpine Valley Music Theater in Alpine Valley, Wisconsin and the Red Rocks Amphitheater in Colorado, thankfully involved fewer cops.

A couple of my buddies were artists so they would sell t-shirts at the shows and I would help them with that, but usually I was going there to have more fun than just making some money selling t-shirts. Those shows were filled with unique people who were so cool and colorful and free of judgment. It was a time and a place where people could really express themselves. And the music was great. But I had my own business. I had responsibilities and had to make sure I was back in Minnesota to meet the demands of my clients, so my travels with the Dead were limited.

To this day I love hearing a Grateful Dead song. I picture an amazing, eclectic crowd of people dancing, and I go right back to the days when I could see them live. If you want to hear someone play just like the Dead, listen to the Dark Star Orchestra. Each show they perform they take some date back in the mid-1970s or whenever, and then re-create it, every song set the Grateful Dead played. The whole game is to try to figure out what night it was that they're recreating. It's a lot of fun.

# Andrea
### 1983 | age 21

The best part of all the hard work I was doing when I was young, was having money to do fun things. Winter of 1983, Pete Simon, Brian Cunningham, Gary Holm, Peter Carlson, Rob Hanzlik and I made our way to Florida where we soaked up the sun, looked for ladies, and paid no attention whatsoever to what we were consuming and putting in our bodies. It was a great adventure with the guys, and shortly after I returned home, I fell in love.

Andrea Copeland was the cute cashier at Surdyk's Liquor store in northeast Minneapolis where I would go buy a flat of Special X beer almost daily. As often as I could I would stand in her line hoping to talk to her.

One evening while she was ringing up my beer purchase, I said, "I've written so many checks here by now you must have my phone number memorized. When you gonna call me?"

"I don't call boys," she said without a blink.

So I asked, "Well, what's your number?"

To my surprise, she gave it to me.

I called her up and we went out to First Street Station on the banks of the Mississippi River. When I met Andrea I was working full-time, taking classes at the University of Minnesota part-time, and living life pretty wild. In that regard, Andrea, the second oldest of twelve, was good for me. She was not living life pretty wild. She was working at a liquor store and taking classes at the U part-time, and she was driven to be successful. She lived in a dorm not far from where I was living in southeast Minneapolis off of Como Avenue. I describe her as a survivor. She was. And is. She was the oldest of 12 children and took on the role of responsibility early in life. A funny and bright woman, she worked hard for her beliefs.

Problem solving and entrepreneurship is in my blood, so in my early 20s, I put it to good use. There was an item on the market called the Furnace Brain. A cool little device I had learned about that could be placed on a gas furnace to cycle the burners so the homeowner would save around 30% a year on their heating bill. The burners today automatically do that, but back then they did not. Then, of course, there were the ten stoves I bought from a school that was closing, and the 500 solar panels I purchased from an overturned semi-truck. That spring and summer, after placing an ad in the Minneapolis Star Tribune, I had regular Saturday morning hours selling stoves and solar panels. I paid a couple hundred bucks for all ten stoves and sold them for a couple hundred bucks a piece. I purchased the 500 solar panels that could be salvaged from the wreckage for $500 and sold them for $50 each. I was making a couple thousand bucks every weekend giving people a real deal on unwanted stoves and slightly damaged solar panels. Knowing Andrea did not have a lot of money or a car, I traded some of the solar panels to buy her a brown Volaré.

For four years, I played around at the University of Minnesota going to school part-time to become an architect. I was really good at math, but having a short attention span, and learning the starting salaries at that time were $16,000 – what I was already making – I decided to be done with college. Unfortunately, I didn't see the benefit of staying in school and earning a degree. I did, however, at a later date go on to receive my real estate agent licensure.

Building upon my craftsman skills I learned from working with my brother Keith, January 1, 1985, I started my own company: Eastwood Construction. And I continued dating Andrea. She had left her job at Surdyk's and had gone to work downtown at Dayton's selling shoes. While working at Dayton's she was recruited by a staffing company in Minneapolis. Andrea worked hard and advanced quickly. I continued with construction and later in 1985 Andrea and I bought a little house in New Brighton and moved in together. We knew living together before marriage wouldn't be at the time, a huge hit with her Catholic family, but not sharing the new adventure wasn't too difficult as Andrea's mother was busy building a huge shelter for homeless people.

# Marriage and Loss
**1988 | age 26**

On May 6, 1988, I married Andrea, my girlfriend of five years. Our loved ones gathered inside Saint Alfonsus Catholic Church in Brooklyn Center to witness before God the two of us saying, "I do." Saint Alfonsus was the church of Andrea's childhood and the place of her parent's worship. Later that month, on Memorial Day weekend, we joined my family for a gathering with loved ones.

That weekend my dad, who was a really good horseshoe player, was having troubles getting his horseshoe to the pin. He would throw it and it would make it halfway. He'd throw it again, and again only get it halfway there. This was a man I have watched throw forty ringers in a row. He had horseshoes in his back yard and he and his friends played them often. My family and I watched and we knew something was very wrong.

Dad told Mom, "Honey, I just can't hold that horseshoe."

She thought maybe he was having some arthritis or carpal tunnel in his hands. Dad loved horseshoes and not being able to hold that shoe really bothered him. He went to see the doctor the first week of July and they told him he had ALS. They prescribed a few more tests. When Dad and Mom went home and started reading about ALS, they were shocked. They didn't realize what ALS was. None of us did.

My dad had spent his days working in the printing industry as a typesetter and later a proofreader at West Publishing Company.

In the early days he handled a lot of hot lead type which was used to create the text we read in books, magazines and newspapers. It's my belief now that our environment and lifestyle very much affect our bodies. I believe that my father's body was very toxic from the chemicals he encountered through this work and that perhaps that played a part in triggering his ALS. In his final days he talked often about the taste of metal in his mouth.

My dad's ALS progressed fast. Every time he went to the doctor they would shorten the time he had left here on earth. The estimation began with three to five years to live. At the next appointment the doctor said more like three years. Pretty soon it was two years.

My father, Charles Richard "Dick" Pollari, lived six months after his ALS diagnosis. He was walking until the day before he died. He had the bulbar onset type of ALS leaving him physically able but weak and suffocating. With great dignity he opted to not be attached to a ventilator which would have kept him alive, but in bed for the duration of his life. At his final appointment, he was given two days to two weeks to live. Three days later, on January 6, 1989, after he had called his friends to tell them he was dying and he loved them, he took his final breath with his wife and all of his children at his bedside. He was 62 years old and his diaphragm gave out. Those final days were tough, but Dad had courage beyond belief, showing no fear. He said many times he had lived a full life. He didn't want our family to have to go through taking care of him. We were glad for him, but devastated. My wife Andrea and I were starting a family, and our children weren't going to know their grandfather. That really shook me.

## The Good in People
**1990 | age 28**

As children we really absorb what our parents do and say, and a lot of what they believe to be true becomes a part of what we believe. Both of my parents were very hard workers. They had an amazing work ethic and career focus. I had that, too.

In 1990, in addition to owning and operating Eastwood Construction, I became part of a multilevel network marketing business, Excel Communications, based out of Dallas, TX. It was one of those deals where you build a customer base and then your customers refer other people and you build a downline. Our product was 10 cents a minute long-distance calling cards, which at the time was a really good deal. Remember, this was before everyone had cell phones and back then everything was metered. Minutes generally cost 25 cents to 40 cents a minute, so a dime per minute was big.

With a couple years of hard work, I developed a nice residual income stream. I was making a few thousand bucks a month from Excel, and I thought I was set. That's quite a bit of money for a young guy. In the end, a year or two later, that company got bought out and my additional income went away. The telecommunications industry changed. I had come on board thinking that was something that would be around a long time, but of course, who would have known long distance would be where it is now? That easy, big income gave me a look at a lifestyle that I liked and wanted. I saw other people who were big in the network industry making a lot of money working part-time. For that reason, I tried a bunch of multi-level marketing companies, but no matter what investment adventure I was exploring at the time, I always stayed in construction. That was my main trade. In case something didn't turn out too well, it was nice to always be able to go back to construction and have people interested in hiring me. I knew what I was doing. I didn't charge too much. I cleaned up after myself. At the time I didn't realize the value those traits brought to the jobs I did, though many times I got tips. When I did receive a tip I was always grateful. One tip in particular I will never forget.

It was a shirt-soaking hot summer day and I had just finished doing a room addition and had plans to go meet the guys at a bar after work. Since it was so hot, I had taken off my t-shirt. As I was leaving the job site the homeowner handed me $300 cash. I thanked him and shoved the cash into the pocket on my t-shirt. As I climbed into my truck, I set my t-shirt on the seat next to me. I was somewhere over by 66th Street, getting on 35W, when I decided since I was going to meet the guys I should hang my t-shirt out the window to dry off a bit. I grabbed it, swung it outside holding onto one corner while I rolled up the window. I didn't make it a mile down the road when it struck me like a lightning bolt, *Crap! The cash!* I had literally just thrown money out the window. I couldn't believe it. Three hundred bucks! Poof, gone!

I got to the bar, grabbed a beer and told the guys what happened.

"Maybe I'll get the cash back," I said. They just laughed.

I'm a believer that if you put good energy out into this world, good energy comes back to you. I decided to put an ad in the lost and found section of the Minneapolis newspaper and you know what? The day after the ad ran I heard from a lady who was following me on that entrance ramp, saw the cash fly out the window, stopped and picked it up. I called her back and she asked, "What kind of truck were you driving?"

"A brown pick-up truck," I told her.

"I've got your money," she said.

There it was, hope when no one thought it was possible. I wanted to give the woman a big kiss. I tried to hand her a fifty dollar bill when I picked up my cash, but she didn't want anything. I had a new reason to trust people and believe good people do still exist. And I had one heck of a story to tell the guys who thought getting back the cash could not be done. Like Kikos Kazantzakis, the Greek philosopher said, "In order to succeed, we must first believe we can."

# Jeffrey
### 1991 | age 29

May 29, 1991, I became a father for the first time when my son, Jeffrey Charles Pollari entered this world. Born during a thunderstorm in a packed hospital with women in the hallway giving birth, nurses confirmed a lot of babies are delivered during low pressure storm systems. Luckily, we had a room. My wife Andrea had a long and difficult time during labor and Jeffrey got stuck so the doctor had to use a plunger on his head which made him look a little like ET. Watching the doctor yank and pull and plunge, I was a little freaked out for a minute, first baby and all. Birth is an amazing thing. I was happy everyone was fine. Thankfully Jeffrey was born a healthy child. I was so excited I didn't even know if we had a boy or girl. About a minute later I heard "It's a boy!"

Jeffrey always smiled and rarely cried. He was curious. He could Houdini his way out of his crib, and often did. He was easy going. He was never really interested in sports, but he loved, and continues to love, books. He is a voracious reader!

As Jeffrey got older he asked a lot of great questions and offered incredible insights to life. He always seemed older than his age. He was an amazing communicator with adults, but didn't relate to the other children his age very well until later in high school. He attended the University of Minnesota Duluth graduating with a degree in Psychology.

Now, my son Jeffrey (who has renamed himself Infinity, "Fin" for short) is 24 years old. Going through the freedom of finding himself, he loves music and art and yoga. From being an uncoordinated little boy, he has become this extremely amazing yoga person with unbelievable grace. Once during a trip to Florida he stood up on part of a pier striking yoga poses, the sunset in the background. I was in awe. It was like a beautiful dance, and my son, Jeffery, he was and is fearless.

# Stress Setting In
## 1992 | age 30

January 26, 1992, during Super Bowl XXVI the Washington Redskins beat the Buffalo Bills at the Hubert H. Humphrey Metrodome in Minneapolis, Minnesota. I was not there. I was somewhere in the air on my way to Mexico on an adults-only vacation Andrea and I decided to take with two other couples from her work. The trip was not what I imagined.

Before our trip, I had been busting my tail 16 hours a day trying to complete a $220,000 restaurant job in downtown Minneapolis. The hope, of course, was to finish before the Super Bowl. Working long hours and worrying about the "before the Super Bowl" deadline, I hadn't been eating much and was, as you can imagine, slightly stressed out. When I plopped down at 5 a.m. in my seat on the airplane heading for Mexico, I had not completed my job, but I had left it in good hands and I was ready to take a breather. Then, somewhere over Texas, my body decided to have a full blown seizure.

Sitting in the third seat of a five-seat row, in the middle of a gigantic airplane, my eyes rolled into the back of my head, my body began convulsing, and I peed my pants. When I became conscious again, Andrea, my wife, was screaming in horror and an announcement was being made over the airplane's loud speaker asking, "Is there a doctor on board?" There was no doctor.

Scared, I sat there for a moment not feeling very well. Then a kind flight attendant came over, helped me retrieve a pair of shorts from my carry-on bag, and escorted me to the back of the plane where I could change my clothes. During such an unexpected and embarrassing experience, I was incredibly grateful to him for the caring and kindness he showed me.

When we landed, I tried to recover by getting some good calories in me. I ate both Andrea's breakfast and mine. Still, I didn't feel 100%. Mexico did not turn out to be the relaxing trip I had envisioned. Nervously, I returned home and went to the neurologist. Several tests and an MRI confirmed I did not have a brain tumor or anything out of sorts, so I returned to life as normal trying to take better care of my health. The first thing I did was start eating Total cereal, because of course Total had all the vitamins and minerals I needed. Or so I thought. Though my father had passed away from ALS, it wasn't until experiencing my own health crisis at 37,000 feet that the importance of caring for my body began to become a priority. And still, I worked too much and probably partied a bit too often thinking *Eh, nothing's gonna happen to me*.

By 1993, I had become part of the very popular telephone card (calling card) craze. The size of a credit card, the plastic card had on it an access telephone number and a pin, and it was used to pay for telephone services like long distance or the cost to use a pay phone. Some companies placed advertising on the cards or featured incredible artwork or famous people's portraits, which made the cards collectible. With the phone card business at its peak, I left Excel Communications and started a phone card company called Provident Worldwide Communications, the only Twin Cities custom phone card company at the time. After a couple years I ended up selling that company to a public company, and then the stock in that public company essentially became worthless as more changes happened in the industry. As they say, "Nothing ventured, nothing gained."

I would never tell you I was good with my money. I would tell you I made a lot of money and I spent a lot of money. I felt rich if I had a hundred bucks. And if I had a hundred bucks, I would share it or invest it in something new. As my friend Phil Roche says, I was always on the "bleeding edge" not the "cutting edge." The bleeding edge is where new technologies and products are still in the "nobody's going to buy that" phase not yet accepted by consumers, but maybe accepted by a few visionaries willing to be the first distributors or users of the product. I've got that sort of visionary mind where I can see the possibilities and I have a million ideas a day. When I look around I don't see a lot of folks inspired to take the sorts of risks I have been known to take in this life. It's neat when I see someone who is character-driven and has an inventor kind of mind. When I had money, I didn't buy clothes and shoes and nice looking cars. What I would do is try to re-invest. My goal as a business guy was to set up a large employee-owned company where I could be not the CEO, but the CVO, the Chief Visionary Officer. My dream was to be the boss everyone hoped for but never got; the guy who gave generously to help the employee's dreams come true.

In 1993, Andrea and I sold our first home in New Brighton to the city. They were building a community center. We moved to a three bedroom split-level home at 913 Harriet in Shoreview near Bobby Thiessen Park. I finished the basement and added a deck. What was most special about that house is that my second son was born when we lived there.

# Joseph
**1994 | age 32**

April 4, 1994, Joseph "Joey" James Pollari was born. Andrea and I had been at St. John's Hospital for about a half-hour all settled in our room when the doctor came in, looked at the nurse and I, looked at Andrea, said, "Okay, I'm just gonna make my rounds, I'll check back," and out of the room he went.

"Isn't he going to check her?" I asked the nurse as I began to walk out of the room too.

"I'll check her," she said. A second later I watched the nurse come running out of the room yelling, "It's coming! It's coming!" as she chased after the doctor down the hallway.

Stepping back into the room, there was Andrea having our baby, his head already showing. I hardly remember any details after that except that I put my hands around his shoulders and was pulling him out when the doctor came back saying, "Keep going, you got it. Keep going."

So I delivered my son, Joey, and cut the cord, and I was the proudest dad. My hands were the first to touch him.

He had the cutest smile and he was so happy right away. He sang before he could talk. We could hear him singing from his crib, and when he got older he knew all the Disney cartoon and movie songs – lyrics too! He was never into football or baseball or soccer, but he loved to act and sing, and he was, and is, an amazing dancer.

Always trying to be supportive, I knew Joey would achieve his dreams of becoming an actor because it was what he wanted to do from the beginning. And now, having had leading roles in two Disney movies, several theater plays, commercials and voice overs, he is a successful actor in Hollywood. And I am still a very proud dad.

# The Growing Years
**1997-2001 | Late 30s**

September 1997, ten years after my father had passed, I had a moving and memorable experience. Princess Diana had just died. Andrea and the boys were gone, so I was home alone. I was sitting on my bed, watching some of the news coverage about Princess Diana's funeral, and I had this overwhelming sense that my father was present; that he was right there at the end of my bed beside me, watching over me and supporting me. This was the first time I felt that his spirit was there. It was nice.

In 1999, with the kids getting older, my mom suggested we move from 913 Harriet to a home she spotted for sale at 470 Lake Wabasso Court. For $230,000, she thought it was a great buy and would be a wonderful place for family celebrations and gatherings. It was beautiful. It had a brick front, a two-story walkout basement and a three-car garage. I put my craftsman skills to work redoing the basement, putting in a home theater, building a game room complete with pool and ping pong tables. I resided. I reroofed. I built a retaining wall, added a three-level deck, and installed a hot tub. In the yard we had a tree house and land that looked over the lake. It was a home that was perfect for entertaining, which I loved to do, but Andrea and I did not often entertain.

In 2001, an opportunity to entertain presented itself when Nick Holbert, one of the salesmen at Eastwood Construction, came to me and told me about a minister, Harold Fait, who was selling 80 acres of raw land in Sandstone, "raw" meaning there was nothing on it but animal trails. Taking the advice of my accountant to invest in property, Nick and I become partners in purchasing the land. The land was located in Pine County, Minnesota, a county unique in that (at least at the time) there were no building permits needed. If we could dream it, we could build it. So I was dreaming big. During the week Nick and I worked at the Eastwood Construction sites collecting materials being discarded from jobs, and most Fridays, after I completed payroll, we would take one or two guys with us north to Sandstone to make our dreams a reality.

Pine Stone Lodge began with the two of us running a string through the dense woods determining the property lines and using a compass and four-wheeler to develop a driveway plan. Soon after, we sketched buildings and a pond. We installed a geothermal heating and cooling system to provide more efficient maintenance, and we used whatever recycled materials we could. Our project became a real labor of love.

I dreamed of a place where people from Minnesota cities could take their children to experience nature: spend time together without a TV, enjoy a bonfire, take a sauna, see the stars and walk through the woods. Nick dreamed of something different than that. Eventually, to develop Pine Stone Lodge the way I envisioned, it became necessary for me to buy out Nick's portion of the property. So I did.

During this time Andrea and I were living separate lives as a couple. She was always taking care of our boys while I was working on the lodge, which she was more than fine with, but I see now where I took advantage of that and I regret doing so. I also regret missing out on that time with my boys. Still, there was great reward in building and watching my vision for Pine Stone Lodge becoming a reality. There is a lot of awe and wonder in that, and a lot of wonderful things have happened there.

# The Big Red Glow
## 2002 | age 40

One of the many incredible things, which I can't completely explain, happened in 2002. Bert, a guy from Eastwood Construction, and I were working for the day at the lodge, digging a man-made pond. It was fall and the leaves were just starting to change, and the maples just starting to turn red. It was the type of peaceful, quiet day where a person could stand in the yard and hear a mouse 100 feet in the woods. But Bert and I weren't standing around. We had rented a big backhoe for a week and had just turned it off after many productive hours. Bert was an excellent operator and we had the perfect slope needed for our dream pond. He climbed off the backhoe and walked up to the lodge to fill his coffee cup—the guy was a chronic coffee drinker.

Sweaty and tired, I was walking alone toward the garage, happy with what we had accomplished, when I saw something in the woods. I stopped. It was just to my right and to the south of where I was standing, and it was coming toward me.

*What is that?* I wondered, staring at this red light moving through the trees. It was big, about 30 feet in diameter, red, and round. It was not perfectly crisp in its circular form, but more of a fuzzy faded-edge circle. It was fast, but I couldn't hear it. There was no sound to it. And it was like a ball of gas or energy. It was like a thing, a being. I didn't feel like it was a large soap bubble or bouncy ball or something that had fallen from the trees. I felt like it was intelligent. I wasn't scared of it at all. I didn't get the feeling that it would harm me in any way. I know it sounds odd, but it got close to me and it stopped like it was hovering there acknowledging me or simply saying hello. I was like a bug to a light, fascinated and unable to take my eyes off this red . . . thing. I wondered: *What are you? Where did you come from? Where are you going? Why are you here?* And phew! As quickly as it had appeared, it disappeared into the woods.

Turning from the garage I ran to the lodge. "Bert! Hey, Bert! Did you see that? That big red glow, did you see it?"

"What? What red glow?"

Bert was in the Lodge facing the other direction. He saw nothing. I had not had anything alcoholic to drink or any other influences in my body. I knew I had just seen something. When I returned to my home in Shoreview I went online and filed a report for a UFO sighting. I really felt like something had just shown me there are things beyond our human physical form. That red plasma ball in the woods was an entity of some sort and it was definitely beautiful, kind and having fun when it charged up and paused by me. Since the experience, I have come to believe the orbs I've seen in my pictures are more than "sun spots."

After filing the report for the UFO sighting, trying to figure out what in this world I had just seen, I told Andrea about the experience. She shook her head and gave the story no merit acting as though I had said, "Hey, hon, can you pass the butter?"

"Mmmm, sure," she said.

But the moment with that red whatever-it-may-have-been meant something. Maybe it meant I was not alone? Maybe it meant I should be having more joy and fun? Maybe, it was what I needed to take notice: Fast. Red. Stop. Pay attention. Things are happening.

# Annie
**2003 | age 41**

There was always ten years between me and my sister Annie, so my childhood memories with her are limited. I do remember when I was five years old, on my way to go sleep with her in the basement, I fell down the stairs, hit a steel pole, split my head open and needed stitches. It was traumatic. After that, my parents carpeted the stairs.

Annie was a cute, crafty, and curly haired girl. She grew up and moved out on her own. In her life she met and married Gordy, had a baby girl, Bonnie, and adopted a toddler, Brian, from Columbia. She became a dental hygienist, and in later years, a nurse. At her 50th birthday party, at my and Andrea's house, my sister Lora thought Annie was off a bit and very emotional. Days later, in July 2003, just as it happened with my father, and also my father's cousin Cal, my sister Annie was diagnosed with ALS.

Annie, like my father, had a lot of exposure to toxins during her work days. I'm guessing the dangers of mercury and X-rays were not on her radar when she was in the process of choosing her profession. How many of us ever think of the toxins we will be exposed to when we are thinking about what job or career will pay the bills? Could such toxins have been a trigger in my dad and my sister's ALS? I think they could. I think toxin exposure should be a consideration for everyone.

After diagnosis Annie struggled for three years, but she did what she could to continue living well. She was a wonderful listener and many days I enjoyed talking to her. Though Annie was battling ALS, we all tried to go about life as normal.

# A Great Loss
### 2004 | age 42

In the Bible, 1 Peter 1:17 reads, "These trials will show that your faith is genuine. It is being tested as fire tests and purifies gold." I was certainly finding myself in a number of trials and what I can tell you is that I know what it is like to want to kill someone. A certain fire ignites when a person you trust betrays you, steals your belongings, empties out your bank account, and takes your identity. I hate to admit it, but I do know what it's like to want to kill someone.

In 2004, at the age of 42, busy with all the jobs going on at Eastwood Construction and my family, I ran an ad in the St. Paul Pioneer Press looking for a foreman for my Sandstone property. A 29-year-old man, who I am respectfully going to refer to as Sam Smith (not his real name) responded and I hired him.

For several months Sam lived and worked at the lodge in Sandstone. A hard worker, he had similar visions regarding what the lodge and the surrounding area could become. We talked about a big greenhouse on the south side and a trail system for handicapped people to get through the Tamarac bog. And we dreamed together of how we might someday add the ability to access the lakes to the experience.

One day Sam explained to me that he could purchase the Waldheim Resort property on Pine Lake, a property that would offer visitors of Pine Stone the opportunity to be on the water. Sam had shown me official bank documents for a large trust fund he would receive when he was 30. But, he couldn't do it until he had the money, and he couldn't get the money until the following year so the property would most likely be gone. It seemed foolish to pass up the opportunity when the man had the money and would get it in less than 12 months. So, I lent him the money for a down payment. At the time I was in the position to help, so I wanted to help. Waldheim Resort was beautiful and I dreamed of all the wonderful memories that families would soon be making there. I was thrilled he now owned it.

As luck would have it, another opportunity presented itself before Sam was able to access his trust fund. His uncle in Buffalo, MN needed to sell his gravel pit. A construction guy, I could see the incredible possibilities a person is presented with when they own their own gravel pit. Plus, the gravel pit would allow for making funds right now. Again I agreed to help Sam out until he was able to access his money and repay me. I had, after all, seen on official bank stationery, the trust fund documentation.

With things at Eastwood under control, and Sam running everything at the lodge, I went with my family to Florida for a Disney Cruise to the Caribbean. We sailed around and enjoyed spending uninterrupted time together. When the cruise was over and we docked again in Florida, I called Diane Thill, my assistant and office manager, to see how things were going in the working world.

"He's taken everything," she said.

"Who's taken everything?" I asked.

"Sam. He's taken everything."

Sam Smith, my foreman, a man I thought was my friend, had emptied my bank accounts, took all the equipment and materials he could, and opened three credit cards in my name. He stole my identity.

When I returned home to Minnesota from the cruise, I spent days and weeks on the telephone trying to navigate the crashing waves of fraud. Well, sometimes, as heart-wrenching as it is, a captain must jump ship. After months of employment hours lost to trying to explain my misfortune, the time had come to cease the convincing and submission of affidavits. I closed the doors on Eastwood Construction and drew up the paperwork to put Pine Stone Lodge up for sale. Then, on my way to the closing of the lodge, my sister Lynn called and said, "Wait! We're in!"

After hearing the vision of what I hoped to do, and knowing my passion for the property and my love for the lodge I built, my sister Lynn, brother-in-law Steve and my mom, Lois, decided to buy it as a business adventure. Lynn really felt she would kick herself later if she let this sacred Sandstone place go. So instead of selling my labor of love to a stranger, April 2, 2004, I closed on the sale of my lodge to stay within my family and it became Pine Stone Lodge, LLC. The closing date had been scheduled for April 1st, but Lynn wouldn't sign papers until April 2nd because she didn't want the deal to be an April Fool's joke.

If there were to be a silver lining to the hell Sam put me through, it would be the blessing that came from my family becoming a part of the Sandstone property and them continuing to develop Pine Stone Lodge. That would be the rainbow after the rain. But my storm clouds hadn't cleared yet. I did go to court with Sam Smith. It was decided he owed me 1.5 million dollars. Before I saw a penny of that money, Sam Smith died by his own hand.

## Starting Over
**2005 | age 43**

After losing my identity, closing the doors on the business I started, and selling my dream property, I was at the lowest point I had ever been in life and there was only one way to go and that was up.

One day while reading the newspaper, I spotted an ad for a large heating and air conditioning company. They were looking for a salesman, and that Friday they were conducting group interviews. I decided I was going.

When I walked into their office, past the gigantic sales board where everyone could see how well everyone else was doing, I thought to myself *this probably isn't for me*. But I had a real connection with the gentleman who conducted the interviews, and because of my experience in the construction trade and my ability to do things like calculate size of heat loss, I was offered and accepted a job.

During my work days, I would visit homeowners at 1, 4 and 7 p.m. "Hey, I'm Kevin. I'm here to give you an estimate on your heating and air conditioning," I would say with a smile.

Some homeowners would kindly say, "Come on in," while others would simply state, "I just want a price." The latter was a bit more difficult, but there was a magic to 2005: with a booming economy and my gifted ability to connect with people, most of the sales I attempted, I closed.

"You hold the pen, I'll move the paper," I'd say, and they would sign for their new heating and air conditioning units.

My first quarter with the company I saw my name at the top of their sales board. By 2006, my sales set the annual company record and I never felt surer of what I was capable of doing. But, my success was not stress-free.

Some days I'd close a $9,200 sale at 7 p.m. By 9 a.m. the next morning, when I would turn my paperwork into my sales manager, I would be asked why the sale wasn't $100 more; $9,200 from people who didn't have $9,200 at the time was not enough. I did not like that part of my job. I did not like selling to customers simply for the sake of making a sale. Sometimes it was questionable whether or not they needed new systems. Sometimes they certainly could have repaired their old ones. At some point, my priority of money and success was trumped by my need to be honest and sincere with the sale, even if that meant sharing with the homeowner all of my knowledge, and not just handing them the pen and moving the paper.

The mission to make a sale even if it was not necessarily what was needed became a problem for me. The loop holes became a problem for me, too. For example, most days this company did not provide the lowest prices in town. But they did have a low price guarantee, like their advertisement said. There's a difference. The words need to be heard carefully.

"How do you do it?" a fellow salesman asked.

"I sell with hugs," I told him.

Despite the discomfort realizing the disservice I was doing by selling a $9,200 unit - a price beyond what needed to be paid, and in many cases far beyond what the person could afford - I continued and remained one of the company's top sales guys. Then, I had a life-changing experience. I had my "Glimpse of Heaven."

# Glimpse of Heaven
## 2005 | age 43

*"For a seed to achieve its greatest expression, it must come completely undone. The shell cracks, its insides come out and everything changes. To someone who doesn't understand growth, it would look like complete destruction."*
— **Cynthia Occelli**

Everything happens for a reason. We meet the people we are meant to meet. We take the path we are meant to take. We look back over the chapters of our lives and we see there was a purpose for the little moments, little nudges, little whispers that offered . . . Heaven is real.

The International Association for Near-Death Studies explains a near-death experience (NDE) as a profound physiological event that may occur to a person close to death or, if not near death, in a situation of physical or emotional crisis. In 2005, at the age of 43, with my sister Annie dying, my marriage failing, and the stress of my sales job swallowing me whole, I consider my "Glimpse of Heaven" a near-death experience: a game changer, a real turn-your-world-upside-down-give-ya-something-to-believe-in moment. After it, I believed. After my Glimpse of Heaven, I was never the same.

Andrea, my wife at the time, had been praying for me. I had been praying for me too.

Andrea and I had married in her parent's church, but afterward we chose our own Catholic church closer to our home in

A SEEKER'S HARVEST

Shoreview. Every Sunday, for nineteen years, I could be found there standing beside Andrea in the back of the church.

When our two sons were born, they were baptized at that same church. The priest explained the purpose, poured the water, acknowledged the supporters, gave his blessing. And our children, too, went to church with us on Sundays. Andrea's desire for our boys to begin a Catholic path through this life went without dispute. Despite the cost of private school, they learned their lessons from the teachers at our Catholic church, just as their mother wanted.

But for me, the Catholic religion did not resonate. I was searching for, but did not find inside the walls of that church, any sort of unconditional love, peace or belonging. That disconnect became a frustration that only worsened after my Glimpse of Heaven, which to this day I struggle to share in a way that comes close to capturing it. My Glimpse of Heaven was just . . . so special.

It happened on a Saturday morning in the fall, my favorite time of year. In an attempt to cope with the many challenges in my life, I had decided, after encouragement from my sister Lynn, to try to learn how to meditate. I ordered John Edward cassette tapes (John Edward the famous medium) and began listening to tape one: How to develop your psychic powers.

On this tape, Edward talks about going on a walk to your favorite place. He explains that on this walk you will shed all your worries and thoughts, and at some point you will be intercepted by an animal. But it was not an animal that intercepted me.

Awake in my home on Lake Wabasso Court in Shoreview, Andrea sleeping by my side, I pushed my pillows behind me, propped myself up, closed my eyes, and in my mind, through the silence of an early Saturday morning, I heard Edward's voice guiding me on a walk. As he said to do on the tape, I envisioned myself at my favorite place: the lodge I was building in Sandstone.

Upright in bed, eyes closed, I saw my feet walking away from the lodge, through the grass, over the colored leaves and sand to what I refer to as the "Ridge Trail," a trail that begins at the edge of the woods surrounding the property of the lodge. I saw myself there, at the start of that trail, beginning to travel into the trees when I was intercepted by . . . a man! He jumped out of the forest, grabbed me by my shirt and said, "Kevin, you've won!"

*I've won? I've won what?* I thought, looking at him, wondering who he was.

A shorter man, with a buzz cut, he had a beard and a tight fitting white button-down shirt. For some reason I believed him to be a missionary. He was very adamant: "You've won! You've won!" And the feeling I had was I had won something *really* big and *really* big things come with responsibilities.

*Had Cindy Crawford fallen in love with me? Was she not in love with me, but had a deep desire to sleep with me? Had I won the 400 million dollar lottery? Was that the thing I won?*

A list of considerations reeled through my mind each one seeming an impossible possibility. The more I thought about what I might have won, the more I filled up with a sense of anxiety that what I had won was so big it would put me in front of the world speaking to accept it.

*"No, that can't be. No, no. That would never happen to me. Maybe I won a contest, but Cindy Crawford doesn't really love me. Cindy Crawford? She would never sleep with someone like me. The lottery? Me? Four hundred million dollars? No way. Not me. No, that can't be it. What? What had I won? What would have me speaking in front of so many people?"*

I was swimming in the uncertainty of *What is happening? Who is this man? What did I win? Why am I going to be speaking to the world?* Suddenly, as if Barbara Eden in one of her episodes of "I Dream of Jeannie" did her genie blink, BOOM! the missionary man and I were no longer on the Ridge Trail.

We were in a bright light, on beautiful, wispy clouds, in a circle. There were no trees, no grass or colored leaves, no Ridge Trail. We were . . . somewhere clear and white and bright. We were standing in a space. A space with a circle. I was seeing what looked like a gathering of thirty-one people. Somehow though, without a word, I knew these figures were not people. Gathered, here in this beautiful bright space, in this circle, were thirty-one souls. This is the part of my experience where words do not seem to work.

In my mind I was standing in this space – this dimension if you will – that the missionary man and I somehow transported to from where we had been standing on the Ridge Trail, in the woods in Sandstone. My hair was a mess and my jeans and t-shirt were dirty. I was filthy from working on the lodge. I was working, not "winning." Winning something big didn't seem right. I didn't feel worthy of a prize or comfortable speaking to a large number of people. Yet, here I was with this man looking at these thirty-one souls; this circle of souls that were not strangers.

Somehow I knew that. Somehow I could feel that each one of these souls knew me. It was as if during the "blink" I had this immediate upload of information that these souls knew who I was, where I came from, what was going on in my life, where I was going.

Instantly, the second I stood near them, I had this knowingness of them knowing me, and loving me unconditionally. I had this knowingness that every one of these souls knew every thought I had ever had, good or bad, every action I had ever taken, good or bad, every . . . everything. How to describe this feeling that I experienced? "Knowingness" is the word that comes to mind. These souls knew my whole life inside and out. They knew my whole life and they loved me anyway. Unconditionally. All of me. Can you imagine?

The very thought of such a rare gift as unconditional love and acceptance without any judgment or expectations created a presence of complete and total peace in my being. I experienced a feeling unlike any I had ever felt before, a feeling that this – here on Earth – is all just a place and there is something greater. And I felt fortunate to be having this experience of being among these souls.

For the souls, I got the feeling that without them saying a word to me about it, for them, it was like: *You're so lucky. I wish I could have had this sort of experience that you are getting right now, this glimpse. I wish I could have had that. I know it's because of what you're going through with your sister and your wife and your work. I know that. You're special. You're here, so you're very special. Boy, I wish I would have gotten a glimpse when I was where you're at.*

*Glimpse? Glimpse of what? Where am I?* I went from this state of feeling anxious thinking *I'm not worthy of winning anything* to this complete feeling of awe and inspiration: *I am lucky to be seeing this. But what is this? How did I get here?*

Among the souls I had this sense of equality that while no

one was better than any other – there was no upper class or lower class - some had done more service of putting others before themselves. Each of them had the same checklist of services they must experience and some had gotten further on that checklist than others. What was clear to me was that "service" was important. The service was what differentiated the souls, and the service was what moved the soul to its level. So, for example: if your soul is required to love itself, provide shelter for the homeless, and give food to the hungry, and it only gives shelter to the homeless, it still needs to experience loving itself and providing food to the hungry. This soul will be on a different level than a soul that has provided shelter for the homeless *and* has given food to the hungry. Does that make sense? It makes sense in my mind when I think of it as a checklist or a board game. Somehow, in this new space, I had an understanding of this whole system for souls and service. I had a sense that *nothing else matters*. Love, compassion, service - that's what is important. That's what I needed to focus on.

Perhaps this was heaven on earth. Among these souls I felt some of my ancestors and relatives present. I also felt souls that I knew were not relatives but were in some way connected to me. One soul, sitting straight across from me and to the right a little bit, felt very much like a grandfather, my grandfather perhaps.

Around this grandfather soul were other souls gathering as if they were honoring him, but not like he was the king or the leader or any more important than any of them. It was that he was just . . . different. They seemed to be respecting the journey this grandfather soul had been on, respecting all that he had learned.

This feeling that I was experiencing of these souls *knowing* me . . . I can't describe this accurately. There are just no right words. After years of thinking about this experience "knowingness" is the best word I can come up with. I felt like every one of these thirty-one souls I was seeing had been watching my every move, my every breath. And they knew how lucky I was – me, this mortal being – to be standing here in this space seeing them. *Was this what I had won, this opportunity to witness these souls and feel this overwhelming joy of unconditional love?*

Still sitting in my bed against my pillows, eyes closed, I began to have this sort of out of body experience. I believe I managed somehow with this exercise from the tape to get myself into a deep meditative state. In my mind, I was watching myself as if I were watching a movie on a television screen.

Bending at the waist I sat down on what I assumed was a chair. I couldn't see a chair, but I felt like I sat on a chair, in this circle, with these souls. And a woman to my left said, "Don't think your wife didn't have something to do with that (me winning)."

*My wife? What did Andrea have to do with me winning anything?*

At the time Andrea and I had been married for nineteen years. We were successful in our careers, in having two great children, in owning a big, beautiful home. We were successful in many things, but we were struggling greatly in our love life. *What did she have to do with me winning? How did these souls know I had won? How did I know they knew?*

There I was sitting in this circle of souls wondering: *What's next?* When out of the corner of my eye I noticed this big glow to my right. Turning to look, about four beings down, a woman leaned forward and smiled at me.

This woman's face was smooth and round and her hair was short. She looked like she could be in her thirties. An average looking woman with a smile that showed her bright white teeth, she was glowing. Our eyes met and I knew, somehow, that she was kind and gentle and warm. And I knew she had something to share with me. I really got this sense that this was a woman who had known me my whole life, a woman who had been following me and caring for me throughout my lifetime. I was interested in finding out what this woman had to share with me. I wanted to know more about her like: *How do you glow? Why did you look and smile at me? Who are you? What do you know that I do not?*

This Glowing Gal got up, passed by me leaving the circle, and I stood up and followed her. We walked down a short trail of clouds and energy and beauty, and up a staircase fifteen stairs to a landing. That's where we stopped and stood. The staircase though, continued twenty stairs up past where we stopped. At the top of the twenty stairs there was an illuminated doorway with this shimmering golden light. I call it, The God Light. It projected peace and love in a way you could just feel it, and I knew on the other side of this entryway was the ultimate destination.

My desire in that moment to walk, run, leap or fly up the stairs to that entryway with this God Light where I was sure I would walk directly into the hands of God for life, was such a force and whole body sensation it was as if standing there still twenty steps away from it was the same as experiencing ten thousand orgasms all at once; as if the closer you got the more unbelievable it would be and feel, and truly, it would be unlike *anything* you have experienced here on this earth.

I was so attracted to this light every part of my being wanted to get past the Glowing Gal and sprint up those twenty stairs to it. But she wouldn't let me go. I had this feeling that once a soul traveled up the stairs to the light, it did not return. Still, I wanted to go. My kids would be fine. Maybe if I went to the light at the top of the stairs, I would be there to greet my sister Annie when she arrived. I nodded my head to the Glowing Gal. *Yes. I want to go to that light.*

"It's not your time," she said.

But I yearned to go to the light anyway.

"Your work isn't done yet," she said.

"My work? Are you kidding me? I want to go."

"No," she motioned.

"Yes. The light, the door" I pleaded.

"Your work isn't done yet," she said.

My work isn't done? *My* work isn't done! I started sobbing and continued pleading, putting on my best sales pitch to go to that light at the top of those stairs. *Work?* I had been working my tail off my whole life. That light – there was some sense of peace about that light and I wanted to go so badly to that place of peace that to me was beyond all words and where God was the eternal place of love and bliss.

Just prior to this Glimpse of Heaven experience, I had read a book about dimensions. Negative energies that have unresolved issues explains that whole area of people who have passed on and not moved very far. It explains how important it is that we "do our work" here on Earth in this lifetime so we can ascend through these other dimensions, which is where I believe I was – in another dimension – and go right to that God Light I was seeing at the top of that staircase.

What was most difficult about my Glimpse of Heaven experience was this feeling similar to arriving at the top of a roller coaster. I was filled with this intense exhilaration of joy and intrigue around these thirty-one souls in this beautiful place where I was experiencing an unconditional love at a level that I personally had never experienced before. And then, having this incredible drive and undeniable desire to do *anything* I could to get up to this God Light, but I couldn't get there. Descending from the top of this joyful ride, quickly, and moving from happiness into a state of being heartsick, my stomach knotted and I was miserable because I had to leave this space where I was and go back because my "work wasn't done yet." I felt I was at the bottom of a rollercoaster ride, having to begin all over again. I feared I might never experience the thrill and awakening of my Glimpse of Heaven again in this lifetime. And that I might never fully understand what it all meant.

No longer hearing John Edward guiding me, or the Glowing Gal denying my pilgrimage to the God Light, I came back into consciousness with "your work isn't done yet." Turning to Andrea, who was still sleeping, I shook her awake, trying desperately to tell her about this unbelievable experience I just had with the walking and the woods and the man and the winning and the circle of souls and the woman who said Andrea had a part in it and the Glowing Gal and the staircase with the God Light and how I wanted to go to it, but I couldn't because my work isn't done. I shared with my wife every detail, and for a few seconds we made a connection. She was happy. I was happy. It was nice. But nice didn't last.

Whatever consideration Andrea had given my Glimpse of Heaven experience, it evaporated when she realized that meditative moments with winning big things and circles of souls and women who speak about wives playing a part before Glowing Gals take husbands up staircases to show them God Lights and remind them work isn't done yet, *do not* exist in her Catholic belief system. Our moment of connectedness ceased, and there I sat beside my wife, who began dismissing my Glimpse of Heaven in the same way my friends had dismissed my Great Knife Throw as a teenager. Frustrated, confused and afraid of what was to come, I didn't know what to do. My sister Annie was still dying. My marriage was still struggling. My muscles in my upper extremities, shoulders and chest were twitching. And evidently, *my work wasn't done yet.*

# Goodbye Annie
### 2006 | age 44

    In 2006, I spoke to Charles McPhee, a nationally syndicated radio host and sleep expert called the "Dream Doctor," to hear his thoughts on my Glimpse of Heaven. McPhee, a graduate from Princeton, had been helping listeners who called in discover the meanings of what they had dreamed about. Though I was not dreaming when my Glimpse of Heaven occurred, I was curious what McPhee would have to say about it. He had a neat show. It was real popular. I shared with him the details of my Glimpse of Heaven asking, "Do you think it was actually a dream?"

    "It doesn't sound like it was a dream, Kevin," he said. "That was a vision."

    Mid-summer I went to see a neurologist about the twitching in my muscles. He told me the twitching was called benign muscle fasciculation. I tried to talk to him about Lyme disease, but he didn't want to hear the word Lyme. While I didn't want to acknowledge it, there was a fear bubbling up in me that the twitches were not benign and they were not Lyme. But, the doctor said they were benign so I was okay with believing that and I convinced myself I just needed to eliminate some stress and the twitching would go away. But first, I had to have back surgery.

    Since the age of eighteen I had embraced chiropractic care believing chiropractors address the actual root of the problem not simply treat the symptoms. However, despite more than 10 years of chiropractic care, my left lumbar and leg was always going numb and chiropractic was no longer an option. After a visit to my doctor, it was discovered that I had a herniated disc and some spinal fluid that had leaked out from my spine onto some of the nerves in my back. I was referred to a surgeon, a tall, thin man who wore a big cowboy hat and snake skin boots, and had a reputation for being the best. With a business to run, a family to care for, and a lodge to build, in February 2006, I had L5 microdiscectomy back surgery. I'm not typically a fan of surgery, but there are times it is necessary and this was one of those times.

The surgery was fairly simple. After two weeks I returned to work. After several months I had fully recovered. I was glad to be free of that pain. Some pain we have no choice but to endure. That same year I shared one of my last gifts with my sister Annie: my craftsmanship.

Working 12-hour days for the big heating and air conditioning company, and considering a career move to a smaller heating and air conditioning company, I was still struggling in my marriage, and my upper chest and arms had started to twitch. I was also losing my sister to ALS and I had constant reminders of the symptoms of ALS onset. Fear from all of this was creeping in and I wondered if I could have what Annie, Cal and Dad had. Could I have ALS? But I kept saying to myself, *I went to a neurologist who told me the twitching was not ALS*. I attributed the annoying muscle movements to a lot of life stress and thought they would go away. I continued living my life. I remodeled my sister's split-level house in Eagan to make it handicap accessible for her wheelchair. I moved her stairway back four feet and put in an elevator that would hopefully make her everyday life a little easier. I was able to spend time with Annie. It became difficult for me to see her losses from the ALS symptoms and the changes she needed to deal with living her final months mostly bed-ridden and unable to speak.

Then on August 3, 2006, another person announced they had ALS: the Dream Doctor, Charles McPhee. After listeners suspected McPhee was drunk because of hoarseness in his voice and occasional slurred words, he told them he had been diagnosed with ALS.

Twenty-seven days later, August 30, 2006, my sister, Anne Louise Pollari Keeler, passed away, the third Pollari family member ALS casualty. At the time of her death she was 55 years old and had lived three years with ALS diagnosis. Non-verbal and in a wheelchair, Annie struggled with her disease and the feeling that life isn't fair. My sister Annie taught me to know that this disease has nothing to do with life being fair. I love my sister Annie very much and believe the moments when I've felt she is near me, she is.

"The Dream Doctor Show" aired for the last time October 20, 2006. A few months later, in the Princeton Alumni Weekly, they ran an essay by Charles McPhee: *"In God's Antechamber: A relentless illness viewed through clear eyes."* In the essay McPhee says, "Despite this grim prognosis, the tidal waves of emotion and panic that first accompanied my diagnosis have retreated. Today I am buoyed along in the currents of a quick-moving river; as they say, you're never more alive than when you're standing next to death. I realize I have entered a new community — the vast legions of people living with illness, cancer and other bad diagnoses — and I am hardly alone. Most dramatic is my liberation from the illusion of time — that there always will be more time to see a friend, to repair a marriage, to spend with a child, to develop a hobby, or to concentrate on one's spiritual life. There will not always be more time, even for those who are healthy. I have learned that in death's mirror, the magic and beauty of life truly are illuminated. My days are rich and full, spent with family, friends, and colleagues. I am still working, but yesterday I bought my daughter a training tricycle a few months early. Her long legs can't touch the pedals yet, but they will soon. It feels good not to be blind."

McPhee's essay resonates with me. "You're never more alive than when you're standing next to death." For me that seems to be the case. With the many undesirable changes I am experiencing with my body, and the realization that there will not always be more time, I find comfort in my belief that we each have a path in life, and that path, no matter how difficult it may be, has a purpose. ALS, for whatever reason, is part of my life's path.

## Endings, New Beginnings and Changes
### 2007 | Age 45

To say I was never again the same after my Glimpse of Heaven is an understatement. But truly, I was never the same Kevin again.

One near death experience (NDE) expert in the Netherlands described a young man who had an experience similar to my Glimpse of Heaven and he came back into his consciousness no longer interested in money or power. What he now wanted more than anything was to simply help people. This story of this man in the Netherlands made perfect sense to me. I, too, found myself no longer having any interest in money or social status or power, and that was proving to be a problem.

Having a purpose is wonderful, but pursuing it is not always easy. The foundation I created to build my life upon – similar to my parents and my wife Andrea – was developed from a mission to be successful. At the time, that meant making all the money I could. Now, that foundation was crumbling.

After my Glimpse of Heaven, and witnessing death around me, I no longer had the heart to sell to someone a $9,200 heating and air conditioning unit they could get somewhere else much cheaper. Or sell a brand new unit to a homeowner when they should simply fix their old one. Since I was working for a company whose main concern was making the most money possible, this made doing my current sales position impossible. Not long after my sister Annie died, I quit my $100,000 sales job at the big heating and air conditioning company, and decided to go work for a smaller company for less money. My motivation for the move was seeing that the smaller company valued doing what was right more than they valued the amount of dollars collected each day. My wife, Andrea, was not pleased with my decision to quit my position.

To top it off, aware the economy was heading in a different direction, I was insistent we sell our $400,000 home while it still had a high value, and move into something smaller. This caused my already shaky marriage to crumble. While Andrea and I may have been in love in 1988, our 19 years together had shifted and reshaped our relationship. She dictated the day and took care of the kids. I did the yard work and fixed all the house problems. We found ourselves simply going through the motions, and in my eyes, her affection toward me and desire to want to hear about and understand any of my feelings, dreams, and what I was going through, was gone. With different ideas of how to raise our children, live our lives, and discover together what life is truly about, the time had come to go our separate ways.

Thankfully, my younger sister, Lynn, had already started down her spiritual path of understanding the ego and social status and money, and she, too, was embracing the belief that our time here on earth is about so much more. Lynn, who was the only person who truly believed the importance of my Glimpse of Heaven and how it impacted my priorities, stepped forward encouraging and supporting me to do what I needed to do for me.

I didn't want or need every second of my day planned out. I didn't want to keep my kids inside and playing video games so their clothes wouldn't get dirty. I didn't want to preserve the clean kitchen and go out for a late night dinner. I didn't want to live to work because I had to pay for a big house and private school. Life is too short not to be lived with passion and happiness. By fall, Andrea and I acknowledged our fire had fizzled and we began preparing to be apart.

My sister Lynn told me about a weekend seminar with national speaker and author, Jim Self. I decided to go, continuing what had now become a spiritual journey and self-help mission. The first session, an introduction to the weekend, was 7-9 p.m. on a

Friday night. With about 50 people in the room, Jim Self began by talking about the Bulgarian rose. Grown mostly in Kazanlak, Bulgaria in what is known as "The Valley of the Roses" — where 85% of the world's rose oil is produced — Bulgarian roses are sought after for their fragrance, purity, and abundant health benefits. Used to make some of the world's most popular perfumes, chocolates, liqueurs and jams, Bulgarian rose oil is referred to in Bulgaria as "liquid gold" because it is very expensive. It takes 1,000 rose blossoms to produce one gram of Bulgarian rose oil. What Jim Self was going to do over the course of the weekend was show us how we could use the Bulgarian rose to make changes in our lives. I was intrigued.

The first thing he had us do was find a partner. I picked a woman standing near me whom I did not know. Once we picked our partners, we faced each other and spread out so we had enough space to stand about six feet apart. Then, he asked that one partner stand still while the other slowly walked towards them. The idea is that there will become a point where it is uncomfortable to get any closer to this person, your partner, whom you do not know. At that point, you stop. My partner and I did what was asked of us and we ended up about two feet apart.

Then, with the help of his assistants, Jim brought to the front of the room several dozen roses. Giving one rose to each couple, he asked that we do the exercise again; standing six feet apart, one person stands still, the other begins to walk toward them. Only this time the people who were walking were supposed to hold their roses straight out in front of them. As they got to their partner, the rose was to be kept halfway between the two people. So, my partner and I did what we were told. The difference this time from the first time we did the exercise, is that we were literally almost face to face; she was comfortable with me, this man she didn't know, being that close to her, so close we were almost kissing this rose.

We returned the roses back to the assistants and found our way back to our chairs where we discussed what just happened. Everything on this planet, Jim explained, has a positive or negative frequency, even our thoughts. For example, the average human being has, let's say, 60 for a frequency number. Someone with a cold may lower their frequency number to 50. A Buddhist monk, more enlightened with positive thoughts and energy, may have a frequency number of 70. Positive thoughts increase one's frequency. Negative thoughts lower one's frequency. On YouTube, Bruce Lipton's "Biology of Belief" essentially shows how our thoughts change our biochemical reactions, with every thought rebuilding our bodies in either a positive or negative way.

The Bulgarian rose has a frequency or vibration of 320 Hz. After the exercise, Jim explained the Bulgarian rose with its high frequency that literally takes our two energy fields — me and my partner — and creates one. The rose unites us.

The evening was done at 9 p.m., but most people didn't leave until 11. A real energy had been created and we were all excited for our weekend together. "From tonight until tomorrow morning," Jim said, "imagine you are holding that rose."

Friday night, after I left, I imagined that rose suspended in air halfway between Andrea and me to see if that would improve communication. The next morning, on my way back to the seminar, I used the idea of the rose between me and the attendant at SuperAmerica. I had a feeling in both instances that imagining the rose was helpful. When I arrived at the seminar Saturday morning, there was a rumble of conversations as everyone talked about more smiles and more connections while they were interacting with other people. For day two, we were learning about frequency and energy fields.

At the time, I was very much a beginner in this whole frequency and energy field stuff. Many of the people attending the seminar were not. What they knew that I didn't yet is that love is the ultimate frequency. It transforms fear. Self-worth, self-love, loving others, it's a powerful thing.

"Imagine," Jim said, "energy flowing up your spine and going up, up, up as high as you can reach above your head and then pouring over the top and running down this invisible shield around you — this field that we all have — and the energy continues to flow down over this shield to the bottom where it travels back up your spine feeding off the energy that we live in."

That weekend I learned each of us has an energy field that is like an upside down pyramid. Our energy goes out, down to a specific spot and back up. After two days of learning and growing with Jim, the seminar came to an end. Before going home, I asked Jim about my muscle twitches and what I might do to help that.

"Do you meditate?" he asked.

"Some," I said.

"Do it more," he suggested.

By mid-summer 2007, there was nothing beautiful or positive about my relationship with Andrea. After filing for divorce, we sold our Lake Wabasso house. Andrea bought a new house and for a few months I lived there and helped her repair the things that needed fixing. Then, for the first time in my life, I moved out and lived alone in an apartment in Roseville on Rice and 36. I had an outdoor pool, an indoor pool and a sauna.

August 23, 2007, my divorce with Andrea was finalized. She got our 401Ks and most of our belongings. I got my lodge and the ability to live my life the way I thought my life should be lived. We shared the greatest parts of us being together: our boys.

Over the Fourth of July that year I was with my mom and siblings at Lake Nebagamon in Wisconsin. My mom owned a condominium there and spent many summer days there. We fished and hiked and we rented kayaks and went to Amnicon Falls, a beautiful 825-acre state park. Then, my brother-in-law Steve and I were in a bar in Lake Nebagamon, a one thousand person village in Douglas County. A woman came up to me and said, "You're the man in the yellow hat. I saw you at Amnicon Falls."

She was right. I was the man wearing the yellow hat. And she was kind and beautiful and loved the outdoors. Her family owned property on the Brule River, so we had stories and adventures we could share, and we enjoyed our time talking. But my divorce wasn't finalized yet. So, I waited for fall when my life with Andrea was officially over, and then I began dating Renae Blomquist. Renae, too, had been married. Five years before I met her, her husband unexpectedly died. What was wonderful and easy about being with Renae was the affection she showed toward me, affection I had been missing for a long time in my marriage. To be with her felt good.

In 2008, trying to keep my company, Ongo Communications, in business, I met Julia McLean. Julia had office equipment for sale listed on Craigslist. I responded to the ad, and when I went to pick up the telephones, I learned she was a doctor of naturopathy. I began discussing the twitching I was having in my muscles with her. After a second trip to her office in St. Louis Park, Julia diagnosed me via hypodermal ultrasonic (an electrodermal energy diagnosis) with Lyme disease and co-infections associated with Lyme. My great outdoor adventures had given me a not-so-welcomed gift.

Most people don't know only half of those infected with Lyme get the bull's eye rash, and only half of the standard blood tests are accurate. Most don't know a negative test result does not mean you do not have Lyme disease. Ticks, mosquitos, fleas and mites can all carry Lyme. With more than 300 symptoms, it doesn't surprise me that it can take 2-3 years for a person to be properly diagnosed.

I did have a bull's eye rash on my stomach at one time, but I disregarded it when it went away. I never went to the doctor or did anything about it until I met Julia. Of course looking back, I should have gone to the doctor to check for Lyme. One of the fastest growing diseases in America, the doctors now understand the importance of antibiotics when a bite or bull's eye rash shows up. If the antibiotics are given within the first 30 days, they will nip Lyme disease in the bud.

If I can give you one bit of advice: DO NOT go into the woods during springtime.

I had always been an outdoorsman spending a lot of time in the woods and I never wore the big brand bug sprays containing DEET. Why would I? Who wants to put that poisonous crap on? I know, it keeps the bugs off, but it soaks into your skin. Think about it: if a bug won't let its body near it, what does the bug know that we don't? What is the bug spray doing to our bodies? I suggest not putting anything on your skin that you wouldn't eat or drink. I'm serious. Ask yourself: Would I drink this? Would I eat this? If the answer is no, consider whether you should feed it to your body.

I have, in the past, tried some of the natural bug sprays and they kind of worked. Really, I just never thought I would get Lyme disease. Other people got ticks. I didn't get ticks. Well, take what you will from what I've learned. What I can tell you is that it's best to never think: "It will never happen to me." Unfortunately, in my life, I've made that mistake a few times.

If you want to learn more about Lyme disease, there's an

excellent book written by Pamela Weintraub, called "Cure Unknown: Inside the Lyme Epidemic." It's worth your time. So is the documentary "Under Our Skin".

To address my Lyme concerns, I saw Julia for a few years. Her protocol, which was a mix of different supplements and tinctures to kill the Lyme bug they call the spirochete bug, helped me when I followed it. But, it was a change that I didn't want to have to make. Julia's protocol was a major time commitment and, for me, hard to follow. What I wanted was an easy fix. There wasn't one.

What is interesting about Julia's diagnosis of Lyme disease is the many published papers about the association of Lyme and ALS. A very high percentage of ALS patients also test positive for having Lyme disease. I don't know if Dad or Annie ever had it, but I suspect Annie did. She also loved the outdoors.

After a year of dating Renae, I moved from my apartment in Roseville to her home in Eden Prairie where I lived with her and her two young daughters. One day, I went to the Eden Prairie Center to work out. I moved the pin in the back of the lat pulldown machine to 90-lbs, walked around to the front, sat down and reached up to pull the overhead bar down, which I had done many times. This time I was not able to move the bar. I tried a few times then I decided my day of working out was done.

Later that same week, at the Mall of America with Renae, on the carpet in the big hallway, I tried to do a cartwheel, which I could always do. But not this day. My arms collapsed, my body crashed down onto my head, and I felt like I could have broken my neck. It was a complete surprise. I got up, and in my own mind said *Whoa!* With my strong arms and body, doing a cartwheel was very easy for me to do, even as an adult. This experience made me realize how weak I was.

That was the beginning of noticing little things in my everyday life that were changing and it was causing me concern. I had been told, though, that it was Lyme, so I chalked it up to the weakening of my immune system. I had trouble focusing, anxiety, joint pain, body aches and fatigue. I was suffering the effects of Lyme disease. I became more aware of the importance of my foods and drinks and focusing on what I was consuming and how it was affecting my body. Like it or not, I was going to have to put in the time and effort and make it a priority. The fear and worry that I was no longer capable to do the simple things I used to do ignited in me a deep desire to travel because Lyme disease was becoming awful and who knew what it would bring into my life.

With two young children and a full-time job, Renae had commitments that kept her from being able to leave for long periods of time to travel. So, six months after I moved in, I decided it would be best for me to move out. I moved into a friend's home on Snail Lake Boulevard and began thinking about where I might like to go.

At the age of 47, I was uncertain what my future looked like. What I did know was how thankful I was for the great gift my parents gave me in my younger years of freedom and rarely, if ever, telling me no. That allowed me the ability to explore and seek and to be open-minded and think of the many possibilities that are out there in this world.

It was absolutely a bummer things didn't work out with Renae, but, a whole world was waiting for me and I was remaining hopeful there was someone perfect in it for me to love. Until then, I was fortunate to be surrounded by really great people and some fun guys also discovering parts of their life journey. Together, we formed our Men's Group.

During Men's Group we'd gather in a trusting space free of judgment (and anyone not directly involved in Men's Group) and share feelings, fears and successes. We came together to quiet our minds and explore our souls. As we'd enter the room, wherever we were gathering, in the background there would be calming, soothing sounds such as a dolphin swimming. We would begin with a 5-10 minute check-in, each person sharing briefly: Here are my feelings, this is what is happening in my life from my perspective. Honesty was the key to the sharing so that each of us could discover something for ourselves and about ourselves. Confidentiality was also important. It was recommended that participants did not share anything that happened in Men's Group with spouses, friends, family or anyone not directly involved in or actively participating in Men's Group. In other words, what happened at Men's Group stayed at Men's Group.

Positive change comes from purging and processing so after

check-in, we would "go to the grid" closing our eyes and envisioning a new landscape as we spent some time meditating and searching within ourselves. Did we have more we would like to share with the group? If so, we took turns sharing. Men's Group, after all, was a tool to help assess what action steps could be taken to make a positive change in each of our lives, and a way to be held accountable. As we transitioned from a state of "going to the grid," two or three individuals would spend 20-30 minutes sharing on a particular subject. We asked people not to speak while others were speaking, and during our time together we didn't offer opinions unless asked. The point was to be authentic in sharing and recognize what was and was not working in our lives so that we could each learn to live our happiest life. We were there to support each other. Men's Group, for me, was a wonderful way to connect with others and build friendships.

For an outdoors guy, used to building and creating and doing, the technology-driven world we live in wasn't a big deal to me at the time. But, being a newly single guy trying to get the swing of this dating thing and stay in touch with family and friends, my oldest son, Jeffrey, helped me to set up a Facebook page.

Over the next few months I went on a couple different dates and then, very much to my surprise, I joined Match.com. I didn't expect much, which seems so perfect now, because when we let go of expectations wonderful things happen. Well, the most wonderful thing in my love life happened: I met Leslie Hitchcock.

# To Love and Be Loved
## 2009 | 47 years old

The classic story used to be "we met in a bar." Nowadays it may be "we met on Match.com." I never imagined I would have a Match.com account, but there I was. And then I saw her. Blonde hair. Big smile. Sparkly eyes. I read Leslie Hitchcock's profile and sent her a wink.

Leslie still beams today when she talks about it, saying: "I got a message that someone had winked at me – you get a little thing in your email, so I thought I would check it out. I went and looked at his profile. He's handsome. I winked back."

I'm not one to send emails back and forth so I told Leslie if there was some interest I'd like to meet. Our first "meet and greet" was on a Thursday in December. We went to Acapulco's restaurant in Maplewood. I walked into the building and spotted her in the waiting room, and there was no playing it cool. I bounced over and said, "Hi!"

A hostess led us to a small table where we enjoyed good conversation, a couple of beers and a plate of nachos. We set up another meeting for Sunday night at Don Pablo's in Roseville.

Sunday night didn't start off quite as smoothly as Thursday. In fact, I was sure Leslie had decided to ditch me after not calling to confirm. Thankfully, that wasn't the case. As it turned out, Leslie had brunch with a gal she had met through a women's group. They had gotten into a conversation that took hours and Leslie had forgotten our date. When she finally called, she apologized up and down and asked if we could still meet. And we did. And just like at Acapulco's, we enjoyed dinner and drinks and good conversation. I deemed the wait worth it.

Leslie grew up in Hibbing, Minnesota as the oldest of three children. Her grandfather ran the Hibbing Tribune for many years. Her father owned a travel agency. Her mother was a chemist. They had a cabin on a lake. They went to the country club. They were involved with politics. Leslie loved to ski. She loved art. She graduated from the University of Minnesota with a degree in Applied Design.

In 2009, Leslie and I were both beginning new chapters. She had just been laid off and was working as an executive assistant. She was finalizing the details of her divorce while living with her daughter Meredith. I was dealing with demoting myself from master craftsman to passionate handyman, a necessity that was not easy. My "second job" included hours of searching for natural antidotes to my Lyme disease, determined to cure my ailments.

As crazy as it sounds, a week after we met, Leslie and I were planning Christmas and New Year's Eve together. I went to her Christmas, she came to mine. Flying by the seat of our pants, we were enjoying every moment of new love – no matter how nuts our children and family thought we were.

The week after Christmas, Leslie and I traveled north to Sandstone, Minnesota to enjoy Pine Stone Lodge. I wanted to share with Leslie the dream I had built. Of everything I've created as a craftsman – sculptures, rounded offices, winding staircases – Pine Stone Lodge is my masterpiece. So, we went up north to usher in a new year with friends.

I had told Leslie about all the people who would come for New Year's Eve. How we would enjoy a sauna and have a fire, and how Tommy and Tim would play their guitars. Leslie, like me, loves music, and like me, Leslie was anxious for a fresh start to a new year with newfound friends and an evening of fun.

New Year's Eve, Leslie and I were at the lodge eager for others to arrive. I was cooking when we heard the first car come down the driveway. It was my friend Tim Rohling.

"It's Tim," I told Leslie. "Could you grab the door?"

When she opened it, I heard Tim say, "Leslie?"

Come to find out, Leslie had worked with Tim in the jewelry industry, but it had been about fifteen years. When I told her stories of my friend Tim, she had no idea it was *that* Tim. Small world.

My friends became her friends and her friends became mine, and the lives Leslie and I had lived separately quickly became woven together as one: Kevin and Leslie.

With a new year upon us, we began to compose a love song of our own. We enjoyed January's music, drinks and dancing. Leslie drummed through getting her divorce finalized and dealing with her job as an executive assistant being terminated during a company downsize. I sang through difficulties of increased fatigue and brain fog, and endured muscles moving and twitching in their own dance. January 9, 2010, Leslie made it official on Facebook: In a relationship with Kevin Pollari. I smiled.

Later that month, I encouraged her to watch "Under Our Skin," a Lyme disease documentary. I had Lyme disease and I wanted her to know what "in a relationship" with me might mean. She asked herself after watching the documentary, "Boy, is this something I really want to get involved in?"

With Leslie being one year separated and in the midst of a complicated divorce, she had made a promise to her dad that she wouldn't get serious or date anyone until he could give his okay. "Maybe we'll just send out a ballot for everybody, ya know, because my picker is off," she joked with him. Well, she didn't send out a ballot and she didn't get her dad's approval first, but when she did talk to him about me he said, "Leslie, you're already in." And she was. Leslie loved me and I loved her right back. She decided I was vibrant, and though I was not 100% healthy, I was a real go-go guy searching and looking for answers, willing to change my lifestyle. She had fun with me and was attracted to me. She was in. I was in, too.

We were going out and doing all the things normal people do. But really, I shouldn't have been. I knew something needed to change, and Leslie was okay with that. She told me I opened her eyes to many things in terms of health and well-being when the two of us would spend hours in front of the computer watching YouTube or doing meditations or taking a sauna in our two-person infrared sauna. We'd go for a walk outside. We'd go snowshoeing. We'd go to the lodge. We were still doing all the things both of us loved to do, and yeah, maybe I wasn't the muscular guy I had previously been, but I wasn't dying. I had a health issue. We were going to figure that out.

In February, we flew to Mesa, Arizona where my mom was living half the year. Trying to eat healthy was hard in the small kitchen in her trailer, but it was warm and we were appreciative of missing the winter back home in Minnesota. We picked fresh oranges, grapefruit and lemons off the trees.

We traveled to Sedona for a few days and hiked the foothills. We spent some time with my mother and her clan of friends from the area, frequenting the VFW for the polka band. We were the youngest couple there. It was entertaining. We danced, had some drinks and laughed.

By March, I had begun wondering if my Lyme was just Lyme or if it was possible I had ALS. Leslie and I went down the path of *No, I had back surgery. Yeah, it's Lyme disease. No, I don't have ALS.* After we returned home from Arizona, we went to Grand Marais on the north shore of Lake Superior to see the waterfalls. I documented our fun with my camera and shared 27 of my favorite shots on my Facebook. I titled the album "With My Love."

When we returned to our home I started looking for handyman work. Since I could use a partner and Leslie had become unemployed, we found ourselves humming along side by side, hammering and painting and detailing. I reminded everyone of my 25 years construction experience and I was thankful I could do the painting jobs. But that doesn't mean I didn't mourn the loss of my abilities to be a top-notch craftsman. The move from crafting beautiful cabinets, entryways and staircases to painting houses, rooms and walls was quite a transition. Leslie made it a bearable one.

With a deepening love, we talked about family and friends, life lessons, and my Lyme disease diagnosis. I told Leslie, too, about Dad and Cal and my sister Annie who had all lost their battles with ALS. That was part of why I was so frustrated with this Lyme and not being able to rid myself of my symptoms. I swore no disease was going to get me, and I was working hard to take care of my body. By now I was sure the Lyme symptoms should be gone. Instead, they were getting worse.

To have some fun, the guys in my Men's Group arranged a weekend up at my lodge. The only planning we did was for each man to handle a meal. Other than that it was an open agenda, but we planned to go deep and share from the heart. The men were more than willing to help out, with my arms and hands being so weak. They helped prepare the food, do the dishes, and anything else I needed.

Still strong enough to hike, we went to the Kettle River five miles away. It's a beautiful park with excellent trails along the river. There's incredible rock formations, and the sounds of the water going over the rock adds to the experience.

Tom set up a rope swing between two large trees and demonstrated it was safe by trying it out first. They then strapped me into a harness and it was, "Here we goooooo!"

We took saunas, had bonfires, and a lot of good times. It was a weekend of soul nurturing and a little bit of "let go" for each of us. It was great to share with no time limit what was happening in life. It was a neat connection with other men to have that I don't think a lot of guys get. There should definitely be more men's groups.

## Leslie's Aha Moment
### 2010 | Age 48

In May 2010, Leslie had what she calls her "Aha Moment." We were in St. Paul at Ester's house. Ester was a woman in her late eighties, preparing to sell her home so she could move into an assisted living apartment. Her home hadn't been touched in years and there was a lot of work to do. We scraped and painted and fixed all the little things. But I wasn't able to hold the hammer. And the screwdriver kept slipping. And painting at Ester's was difficult. Holding that brush to do the edging - I just couldn't do that. Leslie noticed and she had her Aha Moment: Kevin's little quirks are not Lyme.

Still, we didn't talk about it. And honestly, to me, the symptoms at the time were Lyme disease no matter what anyone said. Lyme disease is what I was willing to accept. I just had to get rid of the Lyme then I could get back to holding the screwdriver, the hammer, the edger. Get rid of the Lyme and I could get back to bending wood in oval shaped offices and crafting amazing staircases downtown. We finished Ester's without a word or acknowledging what was to come.

In June, we talked about my symptoms and the possibility of my having Lyme and also ALS. My right arm was weak. For a long time it was just my left arm and my right arm was super strong driving every screw and pounding every nail. My right arm was my wrestling arm. I wasn't half bad. Not many people beat me. When my right arm started to get weak it was devastating. I had kept a good attitude and had been working hard to eat right and drink things that were good for my body. And I had met Leslie, the love of my life. Now, instead of getting better, was I getting worse?

The loss of strength in my right arm took me back because I was hoping that the weakness in my left arm was related to my neck, which doctors had wanted me to do surgery on from using it in too many ways on the job site. I was dismissing the signs to Lyme disease and damage to my spinal cord in the neck region. I figured the Lyme was adding to the aggravations, but now, with my left arm also losing strength, I knew something more was going on; the fasciculations were becoming more frequent. Leslie spent time learning the details of Lyme, and she began to research ALS. I made an appointment for an electromyography (EMG) test, which measures how quickly a person's motor neurons talk to their muscles as well as how quickly an electrical current moves through those same muscles. I scheduled the appointment and continued chugging along.

Friday, July 3, Leslie and I packed for some summer fun and traveled to Lake Nebagamon to celebrate the Fourth. The family cabin my mom used to own was just a few homes away from downtown on the lake. It got to be too much work and upkeep for Mom so she sold it and moved to a new townhome near the boat landing with a beautiful view of the lake. Instead of saying, "we're going to the cabin," we now say, "we're going to the lake." So, we were going to the lake to celebrate the Fourth.

I took great pride in the work that I did. To be a skilled professional capable of magnificent creations one day, and demote myself to laborer the next, well, having to stop doing that type of work was hard. And there I was in Lake Nebagamon, at my mother's, and the baseboards were too heavy for me to carry into the townhome and down the stairs. So my son Jeffrey carried the baseboards and the saw to the basement. I was still able to cut the boards and nail them with an air nailer. And I did that. But then I stood there and I knew: *this will probably be my last job. Forty-eight years old. How is this possible?*

It was the beginning of the weekend, so I didn't want to dwell on it. I decided *Let's get 'er done* and then have some fun. And you know, as a craftsman I had a vision: pay attention to the details, plan and build with passion, create something unique and memorable. I did all of that with my work, and I was going to do that with my life and my new love, Leslie.

On Saturday, July 4, we were only two blocks from the local bar with a patio overlooking the lake. Sometimes they would have live music there, so we went down to the bar and had a drink. We hung out on the deck overlooking the lake and watched the eagles and enjoyed the beautiful view. There was the hustle and bustle of the boat landing right there, so that always provided something to watch with inexperienced people backing their trailer up into the water, and sometimes people yelling at one another. It was entertaining, but mostly we enjoyed family time together.

I was having this feeling of, *Does anyone understand what I'm experiencing and going through?* The next week I was going to go in and I was pretty sure I was going to get diagnosed with ALS, and my family had just been through all of this with Annie and Dad. *What's going to happen with me and Leslie?* I didn't want to know. I didn't want to hear it.

On Sunday, Leslie and I had spent the weekend staying with the others in my mom's townhome in this wide open space with a lot of beds and a small kitchenette. Though no one was leaving that day, we were winding down from our Fourth of July celebrations and all I could think of was, *How do I prepare to tell my Mom and siblings we might, once again, experience ALS?*

Leslie and I hadn't discussed telling others about the worsening twitching and the weakness and the brain fog and the weight loss. We hadn't discussed sharing that I had made an appointment.

Leslie was still downstairs and Mom, Lynn and Keith were around the table. I was standing near the top of the stairs by the railing and I just started saying it out loud. In the moment, I just felt the need. Leslie came up the stairs to the whole family listening to me. She stood by my side as I explained I was worried I had what Dad and Cal and Annie had; I was worried that I had ALS.

The room went quiet, but the looks on the faces could be felt. There were a lot of tears, especially from my nephew Brian, Annie's son. He had these big tears coming down his cheeks as I explained I had scheduled an appointment for the following week with the neurologist, and it would probably confirm what I suspected: ALS. Leslie was surprised I was acknowledging my symptoms and Lyme may now also be ALS. I was surprised, too. It just sort of happened.

# God Bless You
## July 7, 2010 | Day 1

With the twitching and ALS family history, I knew before I set foot inside the clinic. Still, I hoped they wouldn't say it. With every step toward the clinic door I continued telling myself *This is Lyme. I'll get better, it's Lyme. They can cure Lyme.* The life I was building had no room for ALS.

July 7, I checked in at the clinic for my appointment with Dr. Dove, a tall man from Africa, a very sweet guy. Within minutes my name was called and I walked back to the exam room. Dr. Dove took a pen and made two little pen marks on my limbs: one on my hand, one on my elbow. He then thrust a sharp needle into each. With the turn of a dial a jolt of electricity traveled through the needles and through me as Dr. Dove conducted an EMG which measures the amount of electricity that goes through a person's body from point A to point B.

He poked and charted and measured, and he shook his head while he did it. I tried to sit still and breathe. Breathe. Breathe. But I knew. I knew what the test was telling him. I could feel it. I could see it on Dr. Dove. *Not just Lyme disease*, that's what the test was saying. I inhaled deeper, exhaled slower. I breathed.

"Well, the test didn't call for us to check your back, but let's check your back too," he said. And he made the marks, and stuck in the needles, and turned the dial sending the electricity.

After the last probe of my back, he let out a deep sigh,

"You've got it there, too."

I knew, but I asked anyway: "What do you mean?"

"I'm really sorry, Kevin. You have ALS."

And there it was. Confirmed. July 7, 2010, I was officially diagnosed: Kevin Pollari, 48 years old, the fourth Pollari family member to have Amyotrophic Lateral Sclerosis (ALS), estimated 18-30 months to live. My weakness and muscle twitching was ALS. Like my father. Like his cousin, Cal. Like my sister, Annie. Both Dad and Annie were diagnosed with ALS the first part of July too. Despite my positive thinking, my attempts at clean living, my determination that ALS would not get me – despite my efforts, it was ALS. Damn it! I really wanted it to not be.

Dr. Dove shed a few tears. He's a nice guy. I tried not to, but I shed a few tears, too.

Then he gave me some advice: "Get mean."

"What?"

"Get mean, Kevin."

"What do you mean get mean?"

In a soft voice he said, "I don't know what it is, Kevin, but the nicest people get ALS."

That wasn't the first time I had heard the nicest people get this disease. Annie was nice. My dad and Cal were nice. I am a nice guy, too.

I shook Dr. Dove's hand and thanked him for his time, and I walked out of his office noticeably upset. I walked past the reception desk, through the glass doors, out onto the hot pavement in the scorching sun, crying. ALS! It frickin' got me!

I was standing there, at my car, fumbling with the keys in the lock, tears streaming down my cheeks when I heard a woman hollering at me from the entryway of the clinic.

"Mr. Pollari! Mr. Pollari!" she yelled.

"What?" I hollered back as I turned around to look.

"God bless you!" she shouted.

God bless me? God bless me! I wasn't sure why she said it, but she did. Maybe she says that to everyone. Maybe she just thought I needed to hear it that day. Whatever the reason, I didn't like it. Somehow "God bless you" made the diagnosis more real.

With an official diagnosis, there were some people I needed

to tell. Telling people you have ALS is not easy. It's not anyone's fault, but when diagnosed with a disease like ALS – a fatal disease with no known cause or cure – the majority of folks, in the back of their mind, say, *Well, it's fatal, you're dying and there is nothing I can do.* So it feels like when you breathe those *"I have ALS"* words, your friends and family begin saying goodbye.

I lifted my feet from the pavement and climbed into my car. Pulling the door closed, I turned the key and heard the engine start up. Taking a deep breath in, I cried out a little more. Then I picked up my cell phone and called my ex-wife, Andrea, and I told her I needed to talk to my boys and was coming right over. Next I called my ex-girlfriend, Renae.

Weird, I know. Weird things happen in a state of shock. We are tied to people in our lives and just because someone new enters the picture, it doesn't mean we sever all ties to others. I love Leslie with all my heart and it makes sense that she would be my first call. Honestly, saying to Leslie "I have ALS" scared me. What if she left? Telling Renae was safe. Telling Renae would hurt a lot less. Telling Renae would give me a little practice so I could tell Leslie and my sons.

From the clinic I drove to my ex-wife's house to tell my sons. Things were tenuous still so I wasn't in the house. I stood in the driveway and Andrea and my youngest son, Joey, came out into the driveway. Joey was 16 years old. I said, "I was just diagnosed with ALS."

Joey took this news as black and white. For him, you do or you do not have ALS. Joey didn't want to accept ALS would be the death of me, but doctors said I had it, so I had it, and the statistics said I would die from it. Joey hugged me and said, "I'm so sorry."
I hugged him back and said, "I'm sorry too."

My oldest, Jeffrey, was not home. When I did tell him, he heard what I had to say, but was not accepting it. He was not accepting that I had some fatal ALS disease and I was going to die. I was not accepting that either. I was remaining hopeful that there is always that one guy who is the first to overcome the disease, the one guy who figures out something the other guys didn't. The one guy who doesn't lose his battle with ALS.

As I left Andrea's, my heart was heavy. I now had to drive

home and tell Leslie. But Leslie knew, like I knew, what the clinic was going to say. She had been online reading the papers and the facts and the details and the stories. She knew that my weak left arm and my loss in weight and my muscle twitches were the signs of ALS. Still, Leslie needed to hear Dr. Dove's words, "You have ALS." Leslie needed to hear those words that had shaken me to my very core. I pulled into the driveway. I got out of the car. I walked into the house. I stood in front of Leslie, scared for my life. I told her about the test and what Dr. Dove said and we cried. And we chose not to believe everything we heard.

In mid-July, Leslie posted a picture of the two of us at the townhome in Lake Nebagamon on her Facebook page. It made me smile. Despite this ALS diagnosis, she was making a choice to stay with me.

Toward the end of July, Leslie and I had our first appointment at the ALS Specialty Clinic which is a part of the Hennepin County Medical Center. Rather than having me go to a bunch of different specialists – a neurologist, respiratory specialist, social worker, occupational therapist, physical therapist, muscle doctor, and the nurse advocate for the ALS Association – they have them come to me. That's much easier.

In that appointment, Leslie sat by my side while I tried to convince everyone that I had Lyme disease. Then, one of the specialists looked at me and said, "No Kevin, I'm sorry, but you have the symptoms of ALS." And they went in to great detail explaining, "This is not just Lyme disease."

Despite the neurologist confirming I have ALS, what most of us have come to accept as a terminal illness, I was certain I was going to beat this disease. That I was not going to fall victim. That I was going to figure out the problems and find a solution. Despite being diagnosed, I still had my faith, my view of, *"Hey, who knows. I could beat this thing."*

I got angry at the specialists in my appointment. Leslie got angry, too. We felt we were not being heard. We were in denial. We were holding on to hope. I walked out of that office, quit my job and began a crusade.

The next week we went up to Lake Kabetogama. It's part of Voyagers National Park. Having little funds, I had found a room to rent on Craigslist and it turned out to be a single room, all stone, trapper's cabin built on the lake, outfitted with a small kitchen.

Leslie's parents used to take her to Lake Kabetogama, but she hadn't been there in years. Leslie and I needed to escape the people and the prognosis and focus on something positive. Lake Kabetogama was a childhood memory that was good, so we hopped in the car and drove north.

We rented a boat and it had a tiller-style outboard motor. I didn't have the strength in my hands to manage it, but that wasn't going to stop us. Leslie drove our boat. We cruised around and stopped on an island and had a picnic. We laid out in the sun on slabs of rocks with chunks and veins of granite and rose quartz. We met a man named Bill who grew up in the area and knew where all the sandbars, jagged rocks and hot fishing spots were. So we went to Eats-N-Bait, a restaurant and bait store all in one, and bought a fishing license. Then, we fished with Bill. And even though it was difficult for me to hold my fishing pole, I did hold it. I even caught a largemouth bass.

We woke up in the morning hearing the birds and the water and the wind, and many days, our Vitamix making our green smoothies. At night, you could hear the water on the rocks.

One night, we took the boat to Kettle Falls where we had dinner and a few drinks before boating back slowly for 20 miles through the clear, beautiful water enjoying the peace and contentment and listening to the howling wolves and the slapping water against the rocks. We did not talk about the ALS diagnosis. We did not discuss a plan or question what we were going to do. If you had asked us, we would have told you I had Lyme disease and we were working on ridding me of my symptoms. We stayed in our paradise for five days breathing in the beauty of nature. We held on with both hands to the belief that ALS was not going to win.

In August, I attended my Mounds View High School 30th class reunion. It was great to see everybody who attended, and while I wasn't accepting ALS, I wondered if I would get the chance to see them all again.

By the end of August, it was getting hard for me to type and finding a job I could do was becoming much more difficult. Leslie and I moved to an apartment on the East side of St. Paul on Third

Street, kitty corner from a bar. Some friends owned the apartment building and they allowed us to live there in exchange for my consulting services and the installation of new windows in the entire building. Meanwhile, my mom was looking for houses that were handicap accessible or could be converted to it. She knew firsthand what the road ahead looked like for me.

When I was healthy, one of my favorite things to do in my free time was to go to auctions and estate sales scouting for cool old antique items. Now, Leslie and I weren't in need of the things, but we were in need of money. We returned home and began downsizing and liquidating, sorting items to sell a big sale, and planning the annual Pine Stock at Pine Stone Lodge in Sandstone.

After my divorce, when I was single, I started having parties in the fall at the lodge. A neighbor had a pig roaster, so we roasted a pig. I had a big tent, and the party was usually the first week in October when the leaves were at fall peak colors. Beneath the big tent we would have tables and a stage. I had friends who were musicians and they would take the stage and play. More than 100 people would come camp and enjoy the 145 acres of land. It was a great time. After I was diagnosed with ALS, it turned into a fundraiser. It became an annual event filled with a lot of love and support. It helped me then, and it helps me now.

We had a sale in New Brighton. Then we hauled everything that was left up to Sandstone for the big sale and weekend celebration.

With the help of friends, we had a sale from Monday-Friday, and a celebration Saturday-Sunday. We sold two snowmobiles and my 1914 Evinrude outboard motor. The motor is now on display at the old Conoco, I guess. I had a lot of really cool, old stuff. What we didn't sell, we donated. Saturday afternoon, the campers came rolling in and the tents were set up for Pine Stock.

What Leslie quickly learned was that I am a man who needs to keep his mind occupied planning and doing. What I soon learned is that Leslie is a woman who is with me through the thick and the thin of life. From the sales at the rummage sale and the fundraisers at Pine Stock, Leslie and I had enough to pay off my doctor bills and debt, and enough to hold us for a little while. That relieved a lot of stress.

I also applied for social security disability. When you have ALS there is no waiting period, you receive it immediately. Plus, from the time I was in construction I had always carried a disability policy. Turns out that was a good thing. Suddenly income was a non-issue short term. When you're diagnosed with ALS, whether you want it to be Lyme disease or not, you start to look at short-term and say, "Let's live." So Leslie and I started to live and not worry about the future. Occasionally thoughts of *What will we do?* Would creep in and we were faced with whether or not we were going to let them take hold. We chose not to let it. We chose to focus on Lyme and keep going. We asked ourselves, "If today were my last day, what would we do?" and then we did that. Without a doubt, though it was not always easy, I can say it was the right decision. Sleeping was becoming more difficult for me and instead of sleeping I would sit up and research what I could do to slow the progression of ALS symptoms.

The end of October, Leslie and I traveled to Kentucky to see Leslie's dad who was diagnosed with pancreatic cancer and was recovering in the hospital from a Whipple procedure. When we returned home, "Avalon High" starring my son Joey, appeared on the Disney Channel. There was also an article about him in the St. Paul Pioneer Press. I reminded everybody to watch the show and check out the article.

Leslie and I embarked upon some crafting that fall to stay busy. We made stars out of different tree bark and branches, and decorated them with bows and dried flowers. We had a two-day craft bonanza before the fundraiser friends planned.

# Kevin's Crusade of Hope
## The Benefit | 6 months after my diagnosis

My good friend Laura Flaherty suggested and offered to host a fundraiser benefit at their family restaurant. A committee was formed, which included Laura and her husband, Tom, Diane Thill my former personal assistant and good friend, and my buddy Phil Roche, my love Leslie, my sister Lynn, and me. Leslie had put her incredible organizational skills to good use working with Lynn and Diane on the silent auction. Diane is a real "get'er done" kinda gal, and she and Phil made sure contributions could be made with ease by the use of credit cards. The actual fundraiser was ticket sales for a spaghetti dinner which Tom Flaherty had negotiated with a food supplier to donate. Volunteers organized a bake sale, craft sale, raffle and silent auction. I called Tina, a women I knew from high school, and she made Kevin's Crusade t-shirts and sold them.

On December 5, 2010 more than 600 family and friends filled Flaherty's Arden Bowl in Arden Hills, Minnesota gifting a total of $13,000. Talk about an overwhelming outpouring of love.

A benefit for yourself is an odd thing. What I was looking most forward to was seeing so many of the people I knew and loved. I knew there would be quite a few who would show up, but *oh my goodness*. Never did I expect the benefit to become standing room only. It was hard to be encompassed by such love and not get emotional.

December 17, 2010, I celebrated my one year anniversary with Leslie. Time, my friends, is what you make of it. Leslie and I had been together one year, but it felt like we had been loving one another forever.

By the end of 2010, having been diagnosed with Lyme disease and ALS, I had to prioritize my life. Alcohol and sugars were at the bottom. Sugar is a breeding ground for any disease, so it is not good for my body, period. Guess what most alcohol has in it? Yep, sugar. Guess what else? I'm not the only one it isn't good for.

I used to party with the best of 'em. When you stop drinking, no matter what the reason, a lot of things change. For one, I feel a little better on Saturday mornings. I wake up and I'm bright-eyed and bushy-tailed. Having a clear head all the time gives a person a chance to think and grow. Many Saturday mornings in the past that had not been the case. Waking up feeling good is nice. Not having that cycle of drinking, hangover and poor food choices was nice. However, my decision to stop drinking was not without its waves. My closest friends were used to having a beer with me every now and again, and going to the bar and listening to the bands. Not drinking created a shift in my social group. I was breaking habits and leaving my comfort zone. Through guided meditation and essential oils I had a new found perspective, with some regret of losing touch with close friends. But my mission was to clean up my body and get to the root of my ALS. At this point, December 2010, I was still losing weight rapidly, so slowing that was my number one concern. I hadn't figured out yet that I was experiencing leaky gut and everything — good or bad — was running through me with little nutrients being absorbed. It didn't matter if it was a beer or organic berries.

Leslie and I were very excited that two weeks after the benefit my mom found us a house. It had so much potential. My mom saw the potential of transforming it into a home I could grow into as my ALS progressed. At the time, though, Leslie and I hadn't thought of it in that way. We were looking at it as a place to call home.

We moved stuff into our home, but didn't stay in Minnesota long. We packed our bags and piled into Mom's minivan with my son Jeffrey and headed to Arizona to enjoy the sunshine for a bit.

While in Sedona, Leslie received a call that her father was going into hospice. She flew to Louisville to say goodbye to him and stay with her stepmom. She was gone for three weeks. I was fighting with my ex-wife, Andrea, to rewrite our divorce decree so I could enact the accelerated death benefit due to illness and doctor's expectations for how long I might live.

We returned home to Minnesota for one week before we planned to fly to Ecuador. While we were home, I received some very good news from my visit to the ALS clinic. After a very detailed exam conducted by the neurologist, he said I had a "very slow progression." This gives a good indication of how fast the symptoms get worse, so my symptoms would take a while. I was thrilled to hear it. I had cut out all processed foods, food dyes, white bread and was eating 95% organic. I was also trying many detox therapies, and it is my belief that these things were contributing to the slow progression of my ALS symptoms. It was a great thing to hear before packing our bags to leave for Ecuador.

# Adventures Abroad
## Ecuador | 7 months after my diagnosis

It was time to start checking off my bucket list. I had always wanted to go to South America.

We had chosen Ecuador because of a friend who was researching a place in a beautiful setting where a person could retire for less than a thousand dollars a month. She had a book on Ecuador, and I was looking to get away. Ecuador is beautiful, full of adventures and uses the US dollar. I was sold. Gifted some frequent flier miles from my brother Keith, Leslie and I made flight arrangements and packed our bags. We weren't worried where we were going to stay or what we were going to do. Our plan was to wing it and use our travel guides.

We flew into Quito, the capital of Ecuador, which at 9,350 feet is the highest capitol in the world. My legs were strong and ready to climb mountains, but I was losing weight rapidly and my arms were weak. Leslie carried our bags.

Our desire was to get out of the city and go to the mountains, but my sister Lynn had arranged for us to meet Bryan, a child living in poverty whom her daughter Danielle had sponsored for many years.

We stayed in Quito, a city full of history and beauty for a few days. We were able to bring Bryan and his parents on a museum field trip, and bring them shopping, likely a day that Bryan will never forget.

A 3-hour bus ride from Quito is Papallacta, a small village at an altitude of 11,000 feet. The buses, not having good exhaust systems, were really stinky and a bit toxic so we were thankful Papallacta was where we got off. Lush and beautiful, there were hot springs everywhere: 100-108 degree water coming right out of the ground, perfect for year-round hot tubbing.

Close to the equator, the hostel we stayed at, for $12 a night, had three different pools each with different temperatures which we thought was pretty cool. We got settled in and took advantage of the healing benefits of the hot springs natural waters. Watching the cows walk up and down these really steep mountainside, when we're used to seeing cows in fields, I was doing some reflecting wondering if Leslie and I were going to have this great trip only for me to come home and die. My ALS was progressing and I no longer looked like the muscular man I once was. I felt like I was climbing the steepest hills of my life.

The next day, Leslie and I took a cab up a long brick road to about 12,000 feet. There, we got out and walked up to a higher elevation, maybe 14,000 feet. Our arrangement with the taxi driver was to pick us up where we had been dropped off, at the top of the brick road, at four o'clock. That would give us several hours to explore and enjoy this beautiful landscape, which we did. We smiled at the crater lakes, and laughed in the lightning and rain, and loved the gigantic vegetation that looked like wild house plants. I got a little altitude sickness and we were happy to know our taxi would be waiting for us. But there must have been some miscommunication. Our taxi never came back.

Wet, tired, queasy and needing some food, we started walking down the mountain thinking we would meet the taxi along the way. Instead, Leslie and I ended up walking the two miles back to our hostel room. I was exhausted and cold. Our room had no heat. We did have a fire place, but wood was rationed. Leslie helped me put on every dry layer of clothing I had and I crawled into bed where she covered me up with every available blanket. Hot springs were right outside our door, but I was too exhausted to go out. By morning, in the middle of Ecuador, chilled to the bone, I was very sick and scared. I pleaded with the hostel owner to prepare some green soup or help me find some good food my system could handle, and she did. It was wonderful, but was not the right food for me. I was having trouble catching my breath and breathing, and for the first time, Leslie was scared. For the next three days, sick in bed, I watched the cows on the hillside from my hostel room window, and they inspired me to write this poem:

TUMBLING COWS
By Kevin Pollari

As I lay here, the rain falls gently on the roof
High in the Andes Mountains, I hear the sound of a distant woof.
To my amazement, hundreds of cows graze high on the hills
I wonder as I write this, if I took my mineral pills?
First I wonder how a cow can climb so high
Has anyone ever seen a cow tumble down and die?
The green mountain side is very high and steep
If a cow tumbles, will the rancher weep?
I wonder, do any of those cows ever slip?
Do they lose their footing or ever tip?
The grass is wet and the mountain is steep,
Can they really stay up there and sleep?

My three days in bed were an eye-opener to how quickly I was declining and how weak I had become. Dawning on us that the altitude was too much for me, we packed up and decided to descend down the mountain into a lower altitude level where it would be warmer. At the edge of the Andes Mountains, Tena is surrounded by forested hills and is an entry point into the Amazon rainforest. Some call it the poor man's Hawaii. Tena was our next destination.

Perhaps it was good I had three days to reflect on dying because the bus ride to Tena was intense. We were flying down the mountain into the lush Amazon rainforest. The trek to get to Tena was well worth the beauty. And at a lower altitude, my body was warming up and I was feeling much better. The challenge in Tena, with warm temperatures and humidity, would be to not overheat. My health, in its weakened state, was proving to be a challenge.

In a new area, our goal was to get some good food in us. We stayed in a hostel for $16 per room. The room was great. It was big and we had a kitchen and our own bath and free internet. We met a like-minded couple from Australia and together, with limited resources, we made some great meals. We made big salads with vegetables and fruits we purchased at the marked, and had the local standard meal of trout and plantains.

We considered a day trip into the jungle, but already having experienced some obstacles with my health, in fear of what might happen should I get a mosquito bite or worse, a decision was made not to. Instead, we enjoyed the monkeys, trees, plants, flowers and exotic birds in the city park.

In Tena just long enough to recover from the altitude sickness, our next stop was Banos. Banos, in central Ecuador, with a volcano just behind it, was somewhat exciting. Seven years before we arrived, the tourist city was covered in ash three feet deep when the volcano erupted. With temperatures in the 80s during the day and 60s at night, Banos was wonderful. We were able to find a hostel for under $20 each night, and there were about 80 restaurants serving good food at a good price.

There is an abundance of natural hot mineral springs in Banos. The town had three public pools of mineral springs so we went each day, and it would be all native people and us. Most homes had no indoor plumbing, so these public pools also served as public bathing facilities. We were very much a minority, but everyone was welcoming and smiled and it was a very friendly atmosphere.

Waterfalls flow into the city in several places. The main river is called Rio Grande. Just downstream is an absolutely spectacular 350ft waterfall. Banos is surrounded by scenery and a number of possibilities for adventure. We loved it. Plus, we got good food and I was feeling much better. Still, even with all the beauty and the love, I was experiencing a lot of emotions and uncertainty with what my body was doing, and with what it would continue to do. I tried my best not to think about it and be in the present moment of where we were and what we were doing. Me. Leslie. In love in Ecuador.

We enjoyed our time in Banos, and next we took a 12-hour bus ride to the coast. With breathtaking scenery, mud slides, switchbacks, small villages and waterfalls, there was no sleeping during the ride.

Located on Ecuador's Santa Elena peninsula, we arrived at

Montañita, a small beach village known for its surfing. With unique hostels galore, Montañita is a happening place, much less conservative than the rest of the country. I was most excited to know we would have some good food options.

One degree from the equator, Montañita's coast was peppered with surfers from around the world. Weather was mid-70s, humid without a breeze, and the beauty of the beach could be seen with an amazing sunrise and sunsets.

While we were in Montañita, it was Carnival. Carnival in Ecuador and South America as a whole is an event that embodies the merging of different religions, cultures and schools of thought. Preceding the period of Catholic Lent, Carnival is three days of little to no restraint and lots of celebration. People flocked from inland to the coast and Montañita became the desired destination housing thousands of visitors.

Our room rate went from $12 a night to $50 a night during Carnival. Outside our window we saw people in costumes partying all night long for three days. While we had not noticed anyone drinking or smoking in Ecuador, they do during Carnival.

We met some really cool people. We were some of the only Americans in the whole town. Most tourists were from Europe and Australia. We met another couple from Austria at the hostel we were staying at on the beach. The man played guitar and sang. This couple each had a 5-year contract with the school they were working for in Austria. The 5-year contract states that they receive ¾ pay for 4 years, the fifth year they receive payment but they're on sabbatical for a year. They had been on a nine month adventure around the world. Both being teachers, this was something they could afford, which was interesting. And they're encouraged to take trips every five or six years. Europeans always use the word holiday for vacation and their holidays are always three, four, or five week retreats vs. the get-it-all-done-exhaust-yourself-need-a-vacation US vacations.

This couple was a joy to be around. They invited us to Austria. The invitation made me feel sad. I didn't think going to Austria was really going to be a possibility. I was scared and quite certain I was going home and would be homebound and dying.

I did some writing and started to feel like I was stabilizing a bit, but I was still struggling with food. I was missing my Vitamix smoothies and was feeling fatigued. On the beach walking with Leslie, my left leg was really causing some issues. I couldn't walk beside her without bumping into her because I had to pull my left leg around and had foot drop. Walking into town was hard, too. The 10-minute walk exhausted me, and daily naps started to be a necessity.

After staying in town for a few nights experiencing Carnival, we had moved about a half mile down the beach to the Hostal del Sol where we stayed in a second floor honeymoon suite. With a large private deck overlooking the ocean it cost us $32/night. We watched the surfers, listened to the waves, and enjoyed the ocean breeze. Be we didn't anticipate a tsunami.

March 11, 2011, the fourth largest earthquake recorded happened near Japan causing a tsunami with 30 foot waves. More than 15,000 people in Japan died. Ecuador was put on a state of emergency awareness for preventative measure. If the wave left Japan, it would hit Hawaii before Ecuador.

The rumors were that everything from a three to an eight meter wave was going to hit the whole Ecuador coast where we were staying. The president of Ecuador was taking no chances. Before noon, a mandatory evacuation for the entire town had been ordered. Many people jumped on buses and took taxis. We stayed and gathered our essential belongings from our second floor room. Our hostel owner, whose parents started the hostel we were staying at, was holding his head in his hands and I asked if he had insurance.

"No. No insurance," he told me.

The beaches were empty. The people were boarding up their beachside homes and businesses. We were evacuated with our backpacks up the hill to a church that overlooked the town.

No one knew what time the wave would come. Some were saying four o'clock, but no one knew how fast the wave would travel across the ocean or if it would hit Ecuador. We did know Hawaii, also in a state of emergency, would be hit before us.

Away from the beach and up the hill, from an amazing vantage point, we spent the afternoon and evening waiting for the big wave. The sky looked a little different that day. Maybe we enjoyed each other a little more. I don't know for sure. Hawaii was hit with a wave, but no damage was reported.

Around 11 p.m. the roadblocks back to our hostel were removed. Exhausted, we were some of the first people allowed to travel back. On our way, with our backpacks on, we were confronted by some guys who thought we were looters. For a moment we were fearful we would be shot on site, but we were able to convince them we were tourists simply trying to get back to our room. After a long day we were happy to be in our bed.

The next day we enjoyed more of the same beauty as we walked along the beaches and shared some smiles and took trips to town. I had fun chasing the many different species of crabs I saw as they would scurry across the sand luring me away from their holes. I tried to get a good picture of them. Back then I could still take pictures.

Leslie and I spent our evenings in the surf. The tide would go out, and we would have perfect sand beaches to hang out on. March 19, 2011, there was a supermoon where the moon was the closest it had been to Earth since 1993. A bit before, during and after the supermoon, the ocean tide was really high, reaching up and eroding the sands, threatening the stability of some of the places closest to the beach. That was not wonderful, but the moon that night was spectacular. Leslie and I stood in its glow and held hands and pictured our lives in that very moment, in love, believing that anything was still possible.

We spent the remaining week on the beach, then packed up and moved up the coast to Puerto Lopez. Instead of a surf town, Puerto Lopez is a fisherman village. The fish are caught fresh each day and sold at the market with the many other vendors making a living. There are big, beautiful birds that swoop through the skies. And, like the rest of Ecuador, the people are warm and friendly.

For $45/night, we stayed at a world-class hostel on the beach. Our handcrafted cabin was nestled in a huge garden maintained by a team of people. The people were kind. The scenery was breathtaking. The food was wonderful. We wished we could stay longer, but the cabin was available for only a few days, so we did what we could to soak up every second with each other in our own little paradise. We took in the sites at the National Park and made friends with our cab driver named Harley. He also recommended another hostel to stay at. So we stayed two more days.

With Puerto Lopez in the rear view mirror, we traveled 12 hours into the valley to a city called Otavalo. This valley was huge and had snowcapped mountains that were 30 miles apart. The elevation in the city was somewhere around 9,000 ft. and it was covered in this rich organic soil everywhere. We stayed in the most amazing hostel four miles from town out in the country overlooking the valley. It was on the road to Mt. Fuya Fuya, and around us were these gigantic hummingbirds the size of robins. It was breathtaking.

We were also able to go into town a couple days to the market, which Leslie really wanted to visit. It's the largest open market in the country with all these incredible handmade textiles and crafts for sale, and it was set up and taken down every day which was an amazing thing to watch in itself. My stomach was feeling horrible. I can remember being in that market having a problem with constipation, which is real rare for me, but I had taken something a few days earlier for diarrhea, so I was all stuffed up and extremely uncomfortable. I was sad I wasn't able to enjoy as much as I would have liked to if I were feeling better. I went to a restaurant to rest and drink tea while Leslie shopped for gifts to bring home.

On our map we could see one of the highest peaks of this valley was right behind where we were staying and there was a 45 minute trip, over a brick road taking us up to the base of Mt. Fuya Fuya. The day after my 49th birthday, Leslie and I went into the market to find the last of our gifts and a taxi driver willing to take us to the base of the trail head for Mt. Fuya Fuya where there was also a crater lake created by a volcano eruption. With views of volcano peaks, crater lakes and vast valleys, we were told the hike would be worth it.

The taxi driver, knowing he could make some extra money and knowing we could use the help, offered to guide us up to the first summit at 13,000 ft. He even carried both our back packs. When we stopped walking, probably a mile uphill at high altitude, it felt like we walked right up into Heaven. Encompassed in clouds, we could see the valley below and the beauty of nature for miles and miles. It was one of the most spectacular sights Leslie and I had ever seen.

We were leaving the next day to head back to the United States, and we were both aware this could be my last big hike. There was so much uncertainty with my health and my future, and Leslie and I feared I may be going home to die. Then, after coming down from Mt. Fuya Fuya, I took a turn for the worse and worried I might not even make it home.

Our Ecuador trip had been made possible because our plane tickets were gifted to us with some frequent flier miles from my brother Keith and his wife Linda. For this reason we had two major layovers on the way home: a 6 hour layover in Miami and an overnight layover in New York. We had no understanding when booking the trip of how hard those layovers were going to be on me, especially after being in Ecuador. Shaking, cramped and exhausted, I arrived at the Minneapolis airport a complete wreck. I was scared. Leslie was scared.

# Adventures in Juicing
## April 2011 | 9 months after my diagnosis

The day after we returned home from Ecuador, after a little rest, we drove to Sue's in Eagan. Sue is a friend I met through a Meetup group for people with Lyme disease, and the one who told Leslie and I about Ecuador. Standing in her kitchen, I told Sue how great our trip was, but how badly I was now doing.

"I feel so poorly, I'm ready to die," I said.

Sue exploded, "If you could defend yourself, I'd slap the crap out of you. Are you kidding me?"

She then told me all about what she thought was going to be the solution to my ALS troubles: Gerson Therapy, an intense juicing therapy that has helped heal terminally ill cancer patients. She went on to say she had purchased the $2,000 juicer and planned to teach me about the program. Sue felt this was going to heal me, so I wanted to hear more.

As Leslie and I sipped fresh juice, Sue explained the benefits of using a specialized juicer that would squeeze the juice out of a plant vs. chopping it and spinning it. The concept is that by pressing the juice with a hydraulic ram, enzymes usually destroyed in a regular juicer are preserved. With nine glasses of carrot/apple juice each day, and four glasses of green juice on the menu each day, there would be a need, because the juice would detox my body so quickly, for four to five coffee enemas each day. It wouldn't be easy and it wouldn't be fun.

A coffee enema is where you take a special formula of organic coffee and put it in an enema bag and it flows into your rectum and stimulates your bile to detox your liver and helps get all of the detox materials through your liver and kidneys. If you detox all of these things correctly, you shouldn't have severe reactions to detox. So for instance, if someone has cancer and they have radiation and chemo they essentially are killing off bad cells. Where do those bad cells go? They get flooded out by your white blood cells and they can overwhelm your liver. Next thing you know you're very sick. Gerson's theory is that this coffee enema moves all the toxins out of the body safely.

Enzymes are the sparkplugs that get your body to absorb food, so without doing the enemas and having this kind of major nutrition intake, a person could really hurt themselves and possibly cause a coma of the liver. Without coffee enemas only 3-4 glasses of juice could be consumed each day. But if I was going to do this, I wanted to do it. I wanted to get as many toxins out of my body as possible and get back to a healthier state. So, I went to Sue's a couple days each week for juicing and coffee enemas. Then Leslie, Sue and I decided to go to Pine Stone Lodge in Sandstone for six weeks, where we could juice and detox continuously.

Eating organic foods is important, especially strawberries and all fruit. The non-organic fruits get sprayed with pesticides and herbicides which can be very damaging to a person's body. Underground vegetables are a little safer. The farmers don't have to put insecticide on them, but those foods still get the weed killer and fertilizers from the soil. Organic is your healthiest option especially when your body is weakened or sick. There are more nutrients in an organic fruit or vegetable than one that has been treated with pesticides.

It wasn't until I read Dr. Gerson's book that I truly understood the importance of organic due to the soil the plants are growing in. Dr. Gerson, as a young boy, discovered when someone sprayed their garden with a pesticide, his earthworms went away. The soil from which the plants grow determine the health and nutrition of the plant. In a nutshell, organic soil includes all the trace minerals needed to produce a healthy and nutritious plant. These trace minerals *are not* in conventionally grown food, period. But yes, organic is expensive to produce. It's tough to do. You have to rotate your crops and introduce organic compounds such as manure to rebuild the soil as it only takes about four years to leach the field of all the nutrients required to grow that same crop. In today's farms, for example, they grow corn year after year after year in the same field. How? They use fertilizers. Basically you are eating fertilizer. I've read that in the 1950s it was said that America's farmland had been leached of all its natural minerals to grow crops. The whole fertilizer kick all began as far back as the late 1950s. Essentially I was the first TV dinner generation and we're seeing a big difference in people my age who, during their developmental years, had those TV dinners. People like my mother, who, grew up on a farm, without effort, had organic foods growing up, didn't have all these epigenetic mutations introduced to the body. Today, health issues are happening much earlier in people. Instead of it being in their eighties and nineties, it's in their fifties, sixties and seventies.

After endless hours of research, I learned that Roundup is actually made by Monsanto. Initially Roundup was created just to kill weeds, which is bad in itself, but now, in recent years Monsanto has added these aggressive molecules that penetrate into the plant itself so the bugs won't eat it. We humans are ingesting these aggressive molecules. This is why we want to buy organic and have community gardens. To live our healthiest, happiest lives we need to know what exactly is in our foods, how they were grown and what ingredients were in the soil. Anything that does not say organic most likely has been grown using fertilizers and sprays to inhibit weed growth and deter insects from eating the plant. "Naturally grown" doesn't mean the same as organic. For my juicing therapy, we used all organic foods. There's a little organic store in Sandstone called The Organic Carrot, so we purchased most of our foods for our juicing there.

Leslie was not into this juicing adventure. She likes to do a lot of research and process that research, take a little time to review and then finally decide. I didn't have time for that. My symptoms were getting worse and though Sue had not done this before, she seemed to have a good handle on the process and what the possible outcome of juicing could be. Leslie didn't want to judge something I really wanted to try. I really believed it was going to help me detox the spirochete, the Lyme bugs, and rebuild my immune system, my body, and my energy source by nourishing with organic, fresh fruits and vegetables in the form of juice and meals primarily vegetarian. And the detox portion was doing coffee enemas depending upon how much juice I drank.

Understandably, Leslie was not thrilled about this whole juicing and enema process, but was willing to give it a try, for me, and I was grateful. After spending vacations in Sedona, Phoenix, and Ecuador, this was not her ideal scenario. But, she said, "I can do this for you if this is really what you want to do." So we packed and went to the lodge.

Leslie reminds me, "I'm coming off this Nirvana of a vacation and now I'm sitting here with a tube up my honey's ass." Some days she would be on the phone crying to her dad and step mom because this was a real eye-opening experience for her and all of us. The level of commitment it takes to fix and prepare all these juices and meals each day, and give me my supplements, and fit in the coffee enemas, with two people helping, that was pretty much our entire day. It was quite a change of pace from the mountains and the beaches of Ecuador.

After two weeks Leslie lost it and had a total melt down saying, "THIS IS NUTS! This is absolutely nuts. I don't believe this is doing anything for you."

The Gerson Therapy, as wonderful as it is, is primarily for cancer. It does not address people with tummy issues. Unbeknown to us, I had major digestive issues. My flora was way out of balance so I was not digesting or absorbing food or nutrients, which is why I was continuing to drop weight drastically. So, in addition to doing the Gerson Therapy, I needed to eat some other foods to keep my weight up.

Leslie and Sue had done some more digging and had discovered that while the Gerson Therapy is great for people with cancer, it is not maybe the greatest option for people who have ALS. But it was good for ridding the body of Lyme. Either way, I was still losing weight rapidly. Leslie could stand by no longer. She told Sue, "We've invested in this. We've spent hundreds and hundreds of dollars in food and I don't think it's making a change in Kevin for the good." Leslie didn't believe in the program and didn't think it was helping me, and she was done. I was heartbroken. This juicing was my hope. Was Leslie done with the juicing therapy altogether? Was she done with me too? Our time at the lodge doing this intense juicing therapy had been a real life glimpse of what was to come, of my need for assistance with my food and supplements. I loved Leslie and hoped she wasn't leaving. We packed up and ended our time up at the lodge.

Sue helped teach us that a vegetarian diet is wonderful. However, Leslie and I needed a little protein too. We just operate better with it. So, we started to include eggs and continued the juicing and eating three vegetarian meals each day.

Admittedly, Leslie says now that she reacted to the whole Gerson transition kicking and screaming because it was such a different lifestyle for her, and the difficult responsibility of being a caregiver was setting in. We both wanted to be free to do whatever we felt like doing instead of devoting time to slow my ALS progression with the hopes of returning to health. It was demanding, difficult and life-changing for both of us.

On May 8, 2011, "Dream Doctor" Charles McPhee lost his five-year battle with ALS at the age of 49.

Around this time, I had watched Bruce Lipton's YouTube video "The Biology of Belief," and was shifting my energy to focusing on what I was thinking. I think anyone and everyone can benefit from focusing on good thoughts. Slap a smile on your face and pretend if you have to. Before you know it, you'll believe you're happy, happy, happy, and you'll be the happiest person you know. Besides, negative thoughts lower your frequency. You want to keep positive thoughts and a higher vibrational frequency. What I found most intriguing about Lipton's video is that 99.5% of all his patients have underlying issues related to guilt, shame and forgiveness. It's hard to swallow that these things may be a major contributor to their situation, but it's really important to do what we can to reduce stress, forgive others and ourselves, and try to not regret our past. Know it was part of our journey and part of a lesson we needed to learn. Even today I am still working on these things. The power of positive thinking is one of the greatest things to embrace.

The end of May, I put out a request for help. Leslie and I were back in town and needed help with my juicing program, as we were juicing 20 lbs. of organic carrots, apples and greens per day. Plus, I needed some additional meals. Many of my friends responded, and my good friend Laura began helping out by making meals and dropping them off.

Gerson Therapy was providing some hope, but my weight was continuing to drop rapidly even with three meals in addition to the juicing. I was concerned and Leslie was concerned. I was just not absorbing nutrients, which is bad for anyone, but for someone with ALS symptoms, that can lead to a very rapid progression. After feeling so incredibly weak, by June 2011, I stopped the juicing program.

# A Season of Change
## Summer 2011 | 11-13 months after my diagnosis

Despite my focus on positive thinking and my work on letting go and forgiving myself and others, I was having moments where I struggled with my continued weight loss and progression in ALS symptoms. My world was changing fast and I felt out of control.

In June, I posted a note to my Facebook for people to save the date of Saturday, Oct. 1, 2011 for Pine Stock III at Pine Stone Lodge. I was planning good music, delicious food and great company.

That same month, I spoke to the congregation at Spirited United, the church Leslie and I belonged to at the time. It was such a joy to share a piece of my story and see how others could connect to it. Afterward people were thanking me for sharing my Glimpse of Heaven and my ALS journey to this point. It had been one year since my ALS diagnosis and I had lost my ability to write using a pen or pencil. In addition to helping prepare my meals and making sure I got my supplements, Leslie now had to sign my name. My signature was no longer my own.

The beginning of July we took my sons, Jeffrey and Joey, up to Grand Marais. Both my boys are nature lovers and both of them are avid readers. Joey read "Freedom" by Jonathan Franzen. He finished 500 pages that weekend. It was one of the last times I was able to hold my camera. I took a lot of great shots along the rivers.

Joey had just gotten a new camera, so he followed Jeffrey around taking lots of pictures of him: hugging a tree, meditating, standing next to me. Looking at the photos of myself I was actually still really skinny, and I had a brace on my left leg which allowed me to walk pretty steadily and get around pretty well. I could still get into the boat with some help. That was, however, my last boat ride. I suspected it would be and knowing that was hard. I was declining pretty quickly. The trip, though, was great. Joey and Jeffrey were really bonding. One night Leslie and I went to bed early and the two boys stayed up and talked. Joey said it was one of the best brother talks they ever had. The time with them is one of my great memories.

After the north shore Leslie and I went to Lake Nebagamon for the annual Fourth of July Pollari celebration. We had a wonderful time with my mom, sister Lynn and her husband Steve and their sons Dylan and David.

August 20, 2011, I danced my last dance with Leslie during my niece Danielle's wedding. My legs were so weak I could hardly walk 100 feet. So the dancing was exhausting. I knew when we were on the dance floor it would be my last dance. That's a tough thing for a guy who loves music. I wasn't great at dancing, but I had fun. I miss dancing now.

# Finding God in the Grass
### September 2011 | 14 months after my diagnosis

A month later, I was trying another alternative healing therapy, the Rife Machine. It's a machine that uses frequency to kill Lyme bugs. The inventor, Royal Rife, believed that cancer was a virus and he used frequency or light frequency and light to kill cancer bugs. He also discovered other very small microscopic organisms that could be eliminated with frequency. So I was trying to use frequency to kill my Lyme bugs and it was a very tough time for me. I was very much in need of something special, and I got it.

Next to my Glimpse of Heaven, this day was my most spiritual day. Leslie and I were up at Pine Stone Lodge enjoying the last days of summer. With my hands not working that well, I asked Leslie to go get a blanket and lay it out on the lawn so we could lay down in the sun.

She spread the blanket out between the outdoor speakers and we sat down. Back then I could still get down onto the ground by myself. Plopped down on our stomachs, we were enjoying the sunshine and right in front of us there was a four leaf clover. Neither of us had ever truly found a four leaf clover, and at the time we were in need of a little luck, so it was quite a find.

Leslie said, "Is that what I think it is?" pointing in awe. We inspected it to make sure. Then Leslie leaned forward and pulled it from the ground, and we stood up and went in to try and preserve it. That led to a celebration.

The next morning, while Leslie was working on some crafts for the fall sale I went outside. I couldn't really do the crafts with her anymore which was disappointing and emotional for me. I decided to see if I could find another four leaf clover, though I had never been able to find one prior to our luck the day before. I started my search between the outdoor speakers. It made sense. If I were a four leaf clover I would grow between the speakers where I could hear good music. Well, what do you know – to my surprise I found one! I brought it in to show Leslie right away.

"Hey, hon, you won't believe this," I said, holding it up for her to see.

"Keep it safe, okay?" I said to her, and then I went back outside.

I was looking for all the luck I could find and for whatever reason I thought I would check one more time between the speakers to see if there were any more four-leaf clovers. Well, I found another one! I took that one too, into Leslie, asking her to keep it safe. And back outside I went to do a little work

A couple hours later I came in to find the second four leaf clover of the day had wilted. "Honey!" I said, "Do I have to go find another one?"

I went out the front door of the lodge, stepped into the lawn, and though I shouldn't have, and I knew I shouldn't have, I said in my mind, "God, if there is to be a four leaf clover between my toes, I will breathe God in every step I take for the rest of my life."

You shouldn't do that. You shouldn't put God on the spot like that and ask for things. But I was struggling with all I was going through and I really wanted to know he could hear me. It was sort of a: "You're listening, right? You'd show me a four leaf clover to tell me you're listening, wouldn't you?"

And there between my toes was a four-leaf clover. I bent down, plucked it from the ground where it was growing, and felt like a little luck was coming my way. I felt like God was listening.

Did you know for every four-leaf clover found there are 10,000 three-leaf clovers? Four-leaf clovers are 1 in 10,000! I had no idea. The mutation that causes a four lobe leaf structure is rare. For a person to sit down in a clover patch and look for a four-leaf clover, they are lucky to find even one. Many embrace the idea that the leaves stand for faith, hope, love and when there is that fourth one, luck. According to legend, St. Patrick (A.D. 385-461) used the symbol of a "shamrock" (the combination of two Irish Gaelic word parts that mean "little clover" and applies to many three-lobe leaved plants related to clover) during a time when Christianity could only be spread through storytelling, to illustrate the doctrine of the Trinity: Father, Son, Holy Spirit. A shamrock has three leaves, but a single stem. As St. Patrick became more well-known as a holy man, the shamrock also became known as a holy plant. For this reason, the Irish have a tradition that a three leaf clover represents the Holy Trinity: Father, Son and Holy Spirit. When there is a fourth leaf, it represents God's grace. For many, the shamrock is the historic symbol of Irish faith that gives meaning to "luck of the Irish." Irish priests used to believe carrying a shamrock (three-leaf clover) would allow them to see evil spirits in time to get away, while a four-leaf clover offered protection and warded off bad luck. I took my four-leaf clovers as a sign of God letting me know that He was with me and He was listening and I was in His graces.

I tried, but I could no longer plug my camera cord in and download the pictures I had taken of the four-leaf clovers. I was sad. Gerson Therapy didn't work, my ALS progression was slow but still progressing, and I could no longer work on and improve the lodge I had built.

Mid-September Leslie and I purchased someone's personal collection, 50 buckets of agates. Ever since I was a young kid hunting for agates in Maple, I have loved them. I love the lines and the colors and how different each one is. Agates, for me, are special.

When I was 11 years old, I was in fifth grade and there was a kid in my class, Brian Kabola, who was into agates and rocks. I had my own rock polisher so we connected. He had given me some agates of his to polish. To polish rocks takes about a month. I was in the process of polishing his agates when Brian died. He was found hanging in his treehouse. There was an investigation and it was unclear what exactly happened, but they figured he was playing with some ropes and somehow slipped and hung himself. That was the first funeral I ever went to for a friend. I brought his agates with me and asked his mother what I should do with them. She said, "I think Brian would want you to keep them." So I did. Brian was kind and a little bit goofy and he loved agates just like me. I was glad during his short life we had become friends.

I was reflecting a bit on my childhood and past chapters of my life, and I did a little writing about my boys:

Jeffrey
By Kevin Pollari

We were so blessed, that late day in May
When our son Jeffrey was born, he sure made my day!

With a long night we celebrated your arrival, with your smile so bright
It was an experience of a lifetime, you where my golden light

As a baby, you were so curious, loving, and such a joy
Simply said, you were an amazing little boy

Always a smile, always so good and rarely cried
When it comes to new experiences, your eyes were open wide

Curious, sensitive, funny, cute and little
When it came to walking with mom and dad, you wanted to be in the middle

From baby boy to "little man" I loved you soooo much
Years went by and left me so touched

Sensitive and caring are some of your greatest features
When it came to supporting others, you were the loudest in the bleachers

Off to high school, with a great spirit and mind
Without a thought, you were always so kind

Now older, smarter and wise
Making high grades was no surprise

# A SEEKER'S HARVEST

Videogames, girls and the usual things
When you found yourself, you found your wings

Off to college, to see where your heart will go
You didn't need to party, to make your heart glow

Listen to your emotions, be aware what makes you tick
When you really know…. It's like lighting the wick

Follow your heart in all that you do
When not, you will be blue

Your journey will take you far and wide
Remember you are not far from the other side

You make your father oh so proud!

Joey
By Kevin Pollari

The Angels got together to create a Star....
It was decided by all to raise the bar!

The nurse was chasing the doctor down the hall...
God was pulling back the curtain and your
Entrance could not stall!

You smiled for the camera just a few minutes later...
Three days later, at Chili's, you winked at the waiter...

A happy little boy, as cute as could be...
Your actions and expressions told the story of a
special child you see.

You followed your heart on what was your taste...
Books, movies and music filled your space!

You could dance in your crib before you could walk...
And sing out loud before you could even talk!

We could hear you and see you through the crack in the door...
Amazing expressions you showed, we couldn't wait for more!

The lessons you experience while waiting your turn...
Served you well, as you continued to learn

At school you were a leader in oh so many ways...
You enjoyed your homework, and you were in the plays.

Lots of hard work and developing many skills...
Has been a great help, when given the opportunity to do the drill!

The angels and I are smiling with pride not far away...
Know that your dad's love is here to stay.

Memories with friends and family are precious, and I was doing what I could to make more of them. I love watching baseball and was looking forward to seeing a Twins game live. However, after walking from the car to The Loon Café in Minneapolis with Leslie to meet her son and his girlfriend, I was exhausted. It was a nice day. Sunny, hot and we weren't wearing any coats. But I wasn't feeling up to more walking, so I chose to stay at the bar and watch the Minnesota Twins play on TV. Looking back, I wish I had utilized the local ALS chapter's loan closet and borrowed an electric wheelchair, so I could go on those longer walks and go to a baseball game and go to the mall. My ego didn't allow for that. I maybe wouldn't have qualified for a chair of my own yet, but the loan closet would have been a good option if I had been emotionally ready for that.

October 1, 2011, cars and campers, trucks and trailers all rolled down the driveway in Sandstone for the Third Annual Pine Stock. The leaves were bright oranges, reds and yellows. The roasters were cooking pig and turkey. We had the big white tent set up and musicians were taking the stage.

Around dinner time, Leslie and I went up to the stage and personally thanked everyone for coming out for a weekend of fun, and for always showing their love and support. I was still walking then, but many had noticed how skinny I had gotten and how my left hand and arm had changed. I still remember seeing the tears streaming down my buddy Tommy Lundgren's face after Leslie gave her speech. Seeing tears on his face hit home to me that what was happening to my body was real. Later that evening we sat around the bonfire singing songs and hanging out. We lit a couple Chinese wish lanterns and sent them up into the sky. After watching my friends and family enjoy this beautiful place I loved so much, I gave in to my exhaustion and went to bed somewhere around 11 p.m. while friends and family continued to party and dance until after 2 a.m., including my 83-year-old mother. The next morning we all had a huge breakfast together and some people went out walking on the trails through the property.

A couple weeks later, Leslie and I drove to Orlando, Florida to visit Joey while he was filming on the set of "The Inbetweeners."

I was still driving then. I had devised a tool - the handle of a wooden spoon taped with electrical tape to a wrench – to help me start our vehicle. I didn't have the strength or grip to turn just the key, but with the wooden spoon handle I had the leverage to turn it and continue to drive. I like to tease Leslie that even with my disability I was a safer driver than she is, but I'm always thankful she drives me around now. On the way to see Joey we stopped to visit Leslie's dad, Pete, and stepmom, Lori, in Louisville, KY. I had a conversation with Pete about our situations, both being diagnosed with a fatal disease and what it is to be able to say goodbye, yet still be living.

When we returned home from Florida, I returned to my research and found a great YouTube video that explains how the Lyme infections lead to a breakdown of the immune system which is the cause of many diseases (including all the symptoms of ALS) and co-infections to the Lyme spirochetes intruding the tissues and nerves in our bodies. I wasn't giving up yet on the idea that if I could rid my body of Lyme, I could rid my body of these ALS symptoms.

Reluctantly, I did give into the idea that walking everywhere was using a lot of my energy and perhaps it was time for a wheelchair. I think for someone who has walked around most his life, the resistance I had to getting into a wheelchair is normal. Through the ALS clinic and the physical therapist's recommendations, I went to a specialist at the University of Minnesota where they fitted me for a $30,000 electric wheelchair which I was able to order through Medicare. From the time of order to when you receive the wheelchair is about six months. For someone with an ALS diagnosis this is not a good turnaround time. I borrowed a wheelchair from the ALS loan closet to begin trying it out. Thank goodness for the ALS Association for providing me the "loaner" electric wheelchair.

There's a little more than you might think to ordering a wheelchair. In addition to making sure it is a good fit, you want to consider the ability for the wheelchair to move up and down to adjust to different heights like your bed, a counter, a high table or a bar top. This is called the elevator feature, and in my opinion it is definitely something you want. I paid an additional $1,800 not covered by insurance for this elevator feature. I don't regret it. I was wishing I could order a jet engine on my wheelchair too.

In November, I stayed overnight at the hospital to do a sleep study. I arrived at Hennepin County Medical Center around 10:30 p.m. The door was locked and no one would answer, so I had to walk all the way around to another entrance. It was already late and I was tired. I got checked in and they connected about thirty-five wires to different parts of my body to measure everything from eye movement to breathing patterns. Halfway through, exhausted and frustrated, I had a full breakdown telling them, "I need to go home, I'm not going to finish this!" I did finish, but it was brutal. I couldn't sleep. I kept feeling like I couldn't breathe. I was having a major panic attack. What I learned from this experience (and others) was to not wait to do the sleep study. Do it early. Do it before you use a bi-pap. After my sleep study, I met with a pulmonary specialist to go through the findings.

The next week, I underwent more check-ups and testing at the ALS clinic. I was there from 9 a.m. – 3 p.m. and it was a very long day. Overall they said my decline was still slower than most. My lung capacity had declined from 74% last visit to 64%. Leslie and I knew this was a topic for discussion after meeting with the pulmonary specialist the previous week and going through the sleep study. The plan was to use a bi-pap and get a hospital bed to keep me elevated more during the night. Because my diaphragm was weakening, they suggested I get a feeding tube because placing me under anesthesia would become more risky the lower my lung capacity got. My swallowing and talking hadn't been affected much, so I wouldn't really need it all the time but could get more calories and conserve energy for things other than eating. I chose not to get the feeding tube. With my care team I also discussed resources for a ramp and bathroom remodel and talked about implementing "Share the Care," my list of friends and family willing to help. Leslie planned to work with a mentor from the ALS Association to help manage my needs and hers. In addition to our physical and emotional needs, we were becoming very aware of our financial needs.

Money, my friends, does strange things to people. When I was 24 years old I invested in a million dollar life insurance policy through Mass Mutual. In that policy it stated that if you have a letter from a doctor confirming that you have one year or less to live, Mass

Mutual will give you an "accelerated death benefit," which means for people who have a terminal illness, they will give 25% of the total value of what they expect to pay out on your life insurance policy. By November 2011, with my ALS symptoms increasing and my doctor believing very much that I had less than one year to live, he gave me a letter stating this and initiated an enactment of accelerated death benefit for my life insurance policy enabling me to take out a quarter of my million dollar life insurance. My ex-wife was not happy about this. She felt the benefits should go to our boys. But, at that time I wasn't sure how long I would live. I was losing weight, and losing lung capacity at about 10% every four months. At 52% lung capacity, I began researching how low it can go and I found that to be anywhere from 15-25%. If my progression continued at a steady pace, I would have 4-8 months to live. The doctor gave me the letter and I sent it to Mass Mutual. But there was a catch.

In my divorce decree it stated that I had to keep the insurance policy enforced until Joey, my youngest son, was 22. Frankly, I had forgotten about that divorce decree language. This meant that I needed my ex-wife's cooperation to change that paragraph in the decree allowing me to apply for this accelerated death benefit. Getting her to sign off on that was no easy task. For three months, Andrea and I negotiated. It was horrible, and I don't think the stress from this ordeal was very good for my health.

I am a man who is 5'10" so 135 pounds is pretty lean. By mid-December I had lost more than 60 pounds since my ALS diagnosis, and with my symptoms steadily growing, my hope was depleting as quickly as my weight.

In December 2010, for the benefit, my friend Laurie Littlefield, whom I've known since junior high, along with her husband, Dennis, and son, Nick, had baked and pre-sold cookies as part of the bake sale. This year, as a surprise, Laurie and her family continued the cookie sales naming it "Kookies for Kevin." For Laurie "Kookies for Kevin" was a sort of "Secret Santa" gift. She told only her husband and son and the people she sold cookies to that she was doing this. Then one day in December she called and asked if she and Dennis could come over as they had something for me. They said their family wanted to give me something special to look forward to each year so they made "Kookies for Kevin" a yearly event.

As Laurie and Dennis sat at my kitchen table with Leslie and me, she said, "I've already sold some bags of cookies for next year."

I said, "Laurie, I may not be here next year."

She just smiled and said, "Yes you will."

Year after year Leslie and I have been touched by the generosity and kindness of Laurie and her family, and other friends and strangers who have worked on "Kookies for Kevin" or helped with various special events in my honor. You never forget those people who give of their time and talent from their heart.

## Two Years with Leslie
### December 2011 | 17 months after my diagnosis

December 17, 2011, marked my two year anniversary with Leslie. What a ride it had been, and what a blessing. To celebrate, we flew to Washington D.C. to see my sister Lora, her husband Matt, and their daughter Kate. We needed a change of scenery.

Leslie helped me lug the luggage through the airport. It was real difficult to walk. Prior to leaving for the trip, I ordered a leg brace to help with my foot drop and weakening leg muscles. I was watching every step to make sure I didn't take any unnecessary steps. I was walking, but it wasn't easy. In the airport I saw those little motorized carts go by and wondered *How do I get a ride?* I tried to get a seat toward the front of the airplane and that helped, too, with not having to take any more steps then necessary.

This visit to see my sister was different from visits in the past. I could maneuver their house okay with a little clinging to the walls, but during outings like going to the Smithsonian, I had to use a loaner wheelchair and ask someone to push me around. I wasn't ready to have to use it quite yet, but all the stairs and walking around at museums was too much for me.

After a few days, Leslie and I returned home just in time to celebrate Winter Solstice with friends. The shortest day and longest night of the year, we were looking forward to longer and longer days filled with more light and more hope.

At the gathering we went to in Afton, Minnesota, I was invited to be the guest speaker and I talked about my Glimpse of Heaven experience, Lyme and ALS. When I was done, I met a man named Joe Frank.

"Kevin," Joe said to me, "I think I can help you."

I was interested in hearing from anyone who thought they may be able to help me with Lyme or ALS symptoms. "Really?"

Joe continued, "I've got a friend who is a chiropractor by trade, but he's helped hundreds of people with Lyme disease."

Having tried everything I could to get rid of my Lyme and its co-infections, I wanted to hear more about this friend. At the end of the evening Joe agreed to put me in touch with his friend, Allan Lindsley, who was a chiropractor in Eau Claire, Wisconsin. Within a few days, I was scheduled for an appointment and Leslie and I drove to Eau Claire.

My naturopath, Julie McLean had already diagnosed me with having Lyme disease, Dr. Lindsley also conducted his own test. With an energy testing system, he also diagnosed me with Lyme disease and co-infection of Babesiosis, and suggested I take his Lyme protocol which consisted of a series of drops I added to water and drank. Dr. Lindsley also suggested I purchase a Scalar Wave Laser system, a handheld laser that you hold on your skin in one place for two minutes then move it to another place and hold for two minutes. It helps detox the blood, providing pain relief as well as give each cell more energy. Dr. Lindsley was getting one of the lasers for his office, but his office was more than 80 miles each way for me.

Leslie and I drove home and I ordered a laser of my own. I also called Joe to thank him for referring me to Dr. Lindsley. Joe and I became good friends. Joe is one of the few people who has always been encouraging and telling me, "Kevin, I see you walking again."

I was continuing to lose my strength in my arms and hands little by little – and I had a noticeably harder time using my cell phone – but I envisioned myself walking again. That hope kept me searching for a cure and doing everything I could to detox my body and rid myself of toxins.

Another method I began was called Raindrop Therapy. This is a type of massage using essential oils. Typically, massage is helpful, but I was noticing after my massages that instead of feeling revived I was feeling tired and weak. One Saturday morning, after having Raindrop Therapy on Tuesday and Thursday, I did my

weekly strength tests and found that I was, indeed, weaker. Why would I be weaker? I googled
"back massage ALS" and found Dr. Steinblock's YouTube video.

In his video, Dr. Steinblock describes how toxins in your tissues around your spinal cord can be pushed into your spinal cord through a back rub or back massage. I listened to the YouTube and started to have an understanding of this brain/gut connection. These microbes that are used to break down your food in your intestinal track and colon are meant to stay there. When you have leaky gut, these microbes leak into the blood stream and end up also in the brain and central nervous system or spinal cord.

It was while watching Dr. Steinblock's video that I realized I had a "leaky gut" which played a major part in the Gerson Therapy not working as well as it could have. The toxins produced in my own GI tract and colon were leaking into my bloodstream. Then, being in my bloodstream close to my spinal cord, during my back massage these toxins were literally forced into my spine. This is why I was weaker on Saturday after having two back massages. Now, I realize, leaky gut, something I had never heard of before, is a worldwide epidemic. I learned that I needed to add probiotics into my diet, so that started my next research project into the world of probiotics.

I was really having a hard time digesting food. I couldn't digest any dairy at all. It would just slosh and cramp my stomach. Some people show symptoms, some people don't. I was told to get about four or five different probiotics that were available. The best are liquid capsules that are stored in the refrigerator. But, none of them worked. I spent hundreds of dollars on probiotics. I did all sorts of probiotics in pill and capsule form. None of the probiotics or enzymes stopped the leaky gut symptoms of uneasy discomfort and loose stools. The best one – which was something I thought I could never drink again – was a probiotic kefir, which I will tell you about later. Again, it's all about the bugs. You don't want the bad bugs, you want the good bugs in your digestive tract. Probiotics will seal leaky gut. Leaky gut is literally spaces formed between the little fingers that line your digestive track.

December 24, 2011 I posted to my Facebook: "Santa please don't forget, I want two arms and two hands to hug my gal and thank her for loving me so much!"

# New Year, New Challenges
## January 2012 | 18 months after my diagnosis

After New Year's we drove down to Mesa to soak up some sunshine and visit my mom. I was right on the edge of still being able to do my own personal care. Things like taking down my pants and underwear and going to the bathroom were really challenging. I still didn't have my electric wheelchair and I was having difficulty with the three steps going up into my mom's trailer. So, I would decide, *Am I staying down in the yard or going up into the trailer?* and try to limit going in and out.

We hung out in the yard a lot. We went to the VFW. We were the youngest couple there. There were some relatives that would come into town that we would meet with. For a week, Leslie and I went to Sedona. Then, we got word that Leslie's father was not doing well, so we purchased one plane ticket and she flew to Louisville, KY to help her stepmom care for her dad, Pete, who had pancreatic cancer. I was still enduring the emotionally difficult process of negotiating with my ex-wife for funds to live on from my accelerated death benefit, so I stayed back with Mom. Leslie's dad died and I missed his funeral. It's one of those moments that I wonder what could have been possible if neither Andrea nor I was living in the past. If each of us was able to look at that day, that moment and that document and say, "Kevin has ALS. He has less than a year to live. He needs this money to do it." Maybe if it had been that simple, the papers could have been signed immediately and I could have been there beside Leslie at her father's funeral. But, it simply was what it was.

Friends were asking, so I shared an update of where I was with this disease ALS. My voice seemed to be fading so I began recording things that I may want to say using a machine. My legs were very weak. I could walk a block or less with a brace on my left leg. My hands were hanging in there to do the very smallest things and needed help with just about everything. My attitude was ok. I continued to envision myself beating this situation and held tight to the hope I would plateau, but as slow as my progression was, I kept getting weaker.

# Traveling West
## February 2012 | 19 months after my diagnosis

    Finally, after back and forth negotiations wondering if I would ever get my accelerated death benefit and what exactly I was going to do if I did not, my attorney called and said the accelerated death benefit was enacted and he had a check for me. I was awarded $237,000. From that amount $15,000 was spent on legal fees for the three months of negotiations with my ex-wife, plus the money for our children's college funds and other things. What I actually received was $165,000. That may sound like a lot of money, but when you have to make it last a lifetime, it is not.

    Still, at the time, I thought I would never have to worry about money again. Though I was trying not to believe it, I was being told over and over again I wasn't going to live more than a year. My accelerated death benefit made it feel like I could actually go do some things I dreamed about.

    After her father's funeral, Leslie flew from Louisville back to Phoenix and received the good news: the fight for my accelerated death benefit was over. We were excited. Already in a borrowed electric wheelchair with my body continuing to decline and having no idea how long I would live, we decided to do a bit of traveling while I still could. I found a 26 foot travel trailer in Arizona to buy, and I purchased a brown F350 Ford 16-passenger van off of eBay that was handicap accessible. We decided to purchase a van and travel trailer as a potential way to move us around the country.

Otherwise, travel would entail special cabs, hotels and airline arrangements.

We traveled home to Minnesota from Arizona through Telluride where my great-grandma and grandpa were buried and where my Grandma Aune grew up. It was so interesting to stand at my ancestor's grave sites and to see the beautiful mountains above their resting place. It's hard to grasp the life they lived as miners in the late 1800s and early 1900s. After we arrived home to Minnesota, we picked up my son Jeffrey, and took the train to Chicago to pick up the van we purchased. When we arrived in Chicago, the train station was so big and my energy limited, so I asked Jeffrey and Leslie to go ahead and make sure we were going the right way to the entrance before I walked all that way to the wrong part of the station. While I was trying to not be a victim of this disease, I was also trying to be smart and do whatever I could to conserve my energy and make the most of my days.

We took a taxi to pick up the van, which became known as "The Big Turd." The van is heavy duty and equipped with a large Braun lift gate, which allows me to drive my electric wheelchair onto a platform and get raised into the van. It can also haul a 26 ft. travel trailer. In my eyes this "big turd" was a beauty! We drove home from Chicago, dropped off Jeffrey and picked up Scott, our roommate and friend. For 25 years, Scott was one of my employees, and for two years he lived with Leslie and me. He was one of my dear friends who helped with my home remodel to make it handicap accessible. Immediately after coming back from Chicago, Scott, Leslie and I headed to Arizona to pick up our travel trailer.

Once we reached Arizona and picked up the trailer, we loaded it up and took off for the Grand Canyon, Lake Powell, Zion National Park, Arches National Park, and headed north to Colorado, but we chose to not go up into the mountains because my breathing was very labored when up in the higher altitude. So we went through Colorado, Nebraska and on to South Dakota and visited Mount Rushmore and Custer State Park. And then we drove home. We were living in the moment!

Zion was amazing. We spent two weeks there. This was a life-long dream to be in an RV in the mountains, in campgrounds, having all those modern conveniences and being out in nature. I still had the leaky gut and I was really skinny, but there was some huge relief with the negotiations with Andrea being over, money not being a worry, and we were missing winter in Minnesota by enjoying national parks. Leslie and I were in a good place in spite of the disease.

At the time, to walk a hundred feet without becoming completely exhausted was difficult, so once we got the van, I started using the electric wheelchair more. I was also becoming very aware that this ALS journey was not only an outward journey, but an inward one. Every cell of my being – mentally, emotionally, physically and spiritually – was being impacted. If ever there was a time in my life when I was to embrace faith, it was now. I had faith that for whatever reason, this was the path I was meant to take. I had faith that my path had a great purpose, and plateauing – no matter what people believed the outcome would be – was possible. With my body changing, I began to focus on useful modes of feeling and thinking. With the love of God and the presence of positive energies in the universe, I continued marching forward. I began working on letting go of everything negative in my life including forgiving people who had hurt me in the past, and, forgiving myself. And I did what I could to share with others what I was learning about my health.

## Getting Grounded
### March 2012 | 20 months after my diagnosis

Some days, I wondered if I would live to fifty; I wondered if I would celebrate another birthday. March 30, 2012, Leslie lured me into Flaherty's Arden Bowl and as soon as we walked in the crowd began clapping and cheering. I walked to the first chair I could and sat down. It wasn't a very far walk, but it was all I could do. I looked around at the smiling faces and smiled back, and it seemed a bit surreal with everything the doctors were saying to me that I made it to fifty. I had some drinks and shared some laughs with family and friends and I wondered if I would live long enough to celebrate another birthday. Maybe I would. Maybe I wouldn't. What I knew was that night at Flaherty's I felt blessed to be 50 and to have so many great friends and family. They help to keep me "grounded", and they fill me up with positive energy.

Ever hear of earthing? We did a little earthing while we were venturing around state to state. I first heard about earthing from a woman who does Biophotonic Therapy which uses light to neutralize negative emotions providing balance throughout the body. Basically, you hold on to two light rods and have your feet on two glass plates that are hooked up to the computer. This woman told me a lot of people are very sensitive to the electronic wave pollution that's in our air.

We all know the benefits of the sun. Well, there are many benefits of the earth, too. Walking barefoot on the earth or swimming connects you to the earth and releases built-up electromagnetic frequencies (EMFs) in your body. This is called grounding. The higher you are off the ground or the farther you are away from the earth, the more susceptible you are to EMFs or wave pollution. This can be proven with a volt ohm meter and you can go to YouTube and watch how to test for EMFs. Unfortunately, one of the strongest disturbances to our bodies is the 60 Hz electrical system wired through our houses. This is another reason it is so important for us to ground our bodies with the energy of the earth. You will actually see and feel the differences in your home as you go from the basement to the first floor to the second floor.

It wasn't long ago that we all walked on the earth with leather soled shoes or boots. Leather soled shoes will transmit. Rubber soled shoes will not. Concrete will transmit. Asphalt will not. Tile floors will transmit. In the city life, it's extremely hard to get grounded. If you think about it, it was only a couple generations ago that we were on the earth connecting with it all the time. One expert called rubber soled shoes a major health hazard, and a famous cardiologist named Dr. Sinatra is all over YouTube talking about the cardiovascular benefits of grounding.

When we are grounded – our bare feet are on the earth's soil – our bodies do not collect the electronic waves. This is why walking barefoot is such a soothing thing to do. Swimming is also very grounding, and so is taking a shower. Sometimes taking a shower is the only way people get grounded.

I was sleeping on silver threaded sheets that connect to the ground plug that is in every outlet. Your home electrical system has a grounding rod which is typically an 8 foot long copper tube. The ground plug is pounded into the grounding electrode conductor. It's city code to have one. Later, I was advised by someone who tests homes for electromagnetic fields, and he told me not to ground through the electrical system of your house, but to set up your own ground directly outside your bedroom window. So he pounded a grounding rod into the ground outside my bedroom wall. Instead of sleeping on the silver thread sheets he advised that I ground the steel hospital bed instead. The silver threaded sheet was working as an antenna and actually running more electromagnetic currents through me.

Another concern is non thermal electromagnetic radiation

(EMR). Power lines, microwaves, towers, electrical transfer relay stations, smart meters, cell phones and especially smart phones all emit EMR. Smart phones are especially dangerous because microwave towers use smart phones as a relay device regardless if the phone is in use placing a call or not. EMRs do not generate any heat or provide you with any real biophysical means to recognize they're causing harm to you, but there's countless studies showing that EMRs diminish the ability of a body's cells to defend themselves and disrupt the cell's natural ability to produce new cells. Studies in Switzerland show that getting plenty of probiotics can reduce electro-sensitivity.

Mold, fungus and yeast can all react differently under the microscope when exposed to the same EMF environments that we all experience in this modern world. This includes one study that showed a 600 times more neurotoxins generated from mold in the high EMF environment.

You might be wondering what the heck you can do. First, don't put your cell phone to your ear. Use your speaker phone or hands-free device. Second, never sleep with your cell phone on your nightstand or within 6 feet of your head. Because smart phones are always transmitting, power them off when not in use. Unplug your microwave. I also suggest avoiding the use of electric blankets or heating pads.

A recent study in Sweden also showed that if an individual started using a cell phone as a teen, that person's risk of brain cancer is five times greater than that of someone who started using a cell phone as an adult. Sadly, you won't see any of these statistics or health facts shared during commercials or cell phone sales pitches.

I ran into a website where I saw a before and after picture of a live blood analysis, which I was familiar with, and it was a dramatic change within 25 minutes so I looked into it more. A light that clips onto the inside of one of your nostrils, an intranasal laser shines up a person's nasal cavity illuminating every single blood cell in the person's body creating homeostasis in their blood system. The idea is to strengthen the immune system with stable and consistent blood cells enabling lighter, easier breathing. An individual wears the intranasal lascr for twenty-five minutes. In that time every blood cell in your body will pass through your nasal cavity. As a laser, this device is not approved in the U.S., but research has shown LED lights can be programmed to the same frequency as the laser and have the same effects, and an LED light *can* be sold in the US. I bought my intranasal laser out of Canada. Upon receiving it, Leslie and I went to see someone who does live blood analysis testing. We wanted to test our blood before and after we used the intranasal laser to see if what I had read was true. First, we conducted a live blood analysis prior to using the laser. Then, each of us took a turn wearing the nasal laser for twenty-five minutes. When our twenty-five minutes was up, we tested our blood cells again.

What happens during a live blood analysis test is a simple prick of the finger and a small drop of blood is extracted and put onto a slide and put under a high powered microscope and displayed onto a computer. There's still oxygen in that blood, so things are alive and moving.

A live blood analysis shows unprocessed foods in your blood cells. I began doing Live Blood Analysis tests in 2010. By summer of 2012, a blood test showed high levels of B12. I found a YouTube from a doctor that talked about the four types of B12. I was taking B12 in lots of different supplements, but it was not the good B12. Methyl B12 is the best. So, I switched to Methyl B12. During one of my live blood analysis test I also had a personal experience demonstrating how electrical currents affect us. The first time that day that I had my blood drawn it didn't look too bad but didn't look very good either. Usually I would wait about 20 minutes between tests. That day I had a phone call to make, so I went to the other room and grabbed my cell phone from my jacket pocket, and made a call. I came back to the testing room and the tech drew my blood sample. I was shocked to see that my blood had totally changed from the first time to the second, and that person doing the live blood analysis said, "Wow, you are really sensitive to EMFs." My red blood cells were all stuck together like pancakes.

From everything I know, this was a dramatic change. The person who did the live blood analysis was amazed.

Intranasal delivery provides a practical, non-invasive method of bypassing the blood-brain barrier (BBB) to deliver therapeutic agents to the brain and spinal cord. This technology allows drugs that do not cross the BBB to be delivered to the central nervous system within minutes. It also directly delivers drugs that do cross the BBB to the brain, eliminating the need for systemic administration and its potential side effects. This is possible because of the unique connections that the olfactory and trigeminal nerves provide between the brain and external environment. Intranasal delivery does not necessarily require any modification to therapeutic agents.

Also, not only would you see red blood cells, you would see white blood cells which are your clean-up blood cells; they're the "garbage guys." We also saw heavy metals, and the background which is all these little bugs. It looked like dots on a black and white TV. The more of those bugs that you have, the more troubles you have.

## Struggling for Independence
### June 2012 | 23 months after diagnosis

 

While I was beginning to use my electric wheelchair a lot of the time, I could still use my walker and climb stairs. However, by the end of May, climbing stairs was proving to be difficult, too. So, we began the demo work on our house to transform two bedrooms into a handicap accessible bedroom and bathroom, and add a wheelchair ramp onto the front of the house. To save money, Scott did a major part of the remodel and I hired people from Craigslist.

I had always been proud to be an independent guy, able to do things on my own, but ALS had slowly been stripping away my independence. I was not okay with my inability to go to the bathroom alone anymore. I couldn't unzip my pants or pull them down. To help me, Leslie sewed a fabric ring onto all my zippers so I could slide my thumb into the ring and pull the ring and my zipper down. She sewed the same sort of rings onto my underwear too. When that no longer worked, at home and in public, Leslie would just come into the bathroom and help me.

My hands weren't working, but most of my other parts were. That's one thing that is very different about ALS: your, ah, "particulars" are not affected. Certain muscles work and certain muscles don't. That always adds a different dimension when you are talking about ALS because guess what? Thankfully, I can still be intimate. So Leslie and I still have our intimacy, but it is different. There is a struggle for Leslie on how to emotionally bounce between caregiver and lover. That's not always easy for either of us.

In late June, I sat down to do a little research and I was very sad when I couldn't get up by myself from my chair in front of my computer. I overdid it the day before and my legs were not working too well.

Determined to keep my independence and walk whenever possible, I had continued to use my walker as often as I could. However, in July while trying to maneuver with it, I fell.

My decline was taking a bit of a toll so we packed our bags and spent some time in Tofte on the shore of Lake Superior. Then we went to a little campground called Top O' the Morn. In northern Wisconsin near Lake Nebagamon to celebrate life and the Fourth of July.

After returning from vacation I began looking at all the things I still owned and started to see a value in selling some of them. Mid-July, my son Jeffrey and I posted our first for sale item on eBay: a Bud Chapman "infamous 18" phone card press sheet. It was a very unique and cool item that I just didn't need anymore. I was looking for someone who collected Bud Chapman's artwork and would like it.

Not being able to do a lot of the things I used to do so well, I wanted to spend a few days with family and friends, so I reminded everyone on Facebook to mark Saturday, October 7th, 2012 on their calendars for Pine Stock IV up in Sandstone. Live music, food, drinks, friends, it was sure to be a weekend of fun and that, at the moment, sounded fabulous. However, by late August, I cancelled the party. Leslie and I had been working hard on our home remodel and my ALS symptoms were progressing. I wanted to do some more traveling while I still could.

Leslie and I took the van and travel trailer up to Grand Marais for two weeks to bask in the beauty of nature. We met up with our friends Bruce, Jim, Geoff and Patty, and enjoyed the MPR Mountain Stage live performance at the Grand Marais Music Festival. To address my struggles with going up and down stairs into and out of the trailer, we had set up a pulley system using a rope that went under my arms and with the help of Leslie would stabilize and guide me up the steps and into the trailer. But we knew this might be the last time I would get to use the travel trailer. With my symptoms worsening, the process was becoming too difficult and not safe for me. Still, my progression was slow and I believed I was doing some things that were contributing to that. In late September, I posted my first video to YouTube to share with others how I believed I was slowing the process of this ALS disease by doing chelation and eating organic foods. If I could, I wanted to help someone else who may just be getting diagnosed or simply struggling with their health.

The third Thursday of each month, the Hennepin County Medical Center has an ALS support group. Though there are hundreds of ALS patients, few attend the support group which is too bad because ALS can be a very lonely disease that causes people to withdraw, which is understandable when the diagnosis comes with little to no hope. With Leslie and I doing a lot of traveling, we rarely attended the support group in the first few years. Sometimes we attend now.

Typically, the ALS support group in the Minneapolis area consists of about 20 people. I imagine the support groups in small towns might be only two or three people. That could be challenging. In the group I attend, people introduce themselves, say when they were diagnosed, and then share a little about what is going on with their progression and what is helping them cope. Sometimes new members seem a bit shocked to see a room full of people in wheelchairs at different stages in their ALS journey. Leslie and I were a little shocked when we first came to a meeting. Many members are unable to talk. Some have full-time caretakers who accompany them. Everyone's progression moves at a different pace so each person's situation is different. For me, in the fall of 2012, I was declining more quickly with leaky gut and Lyme disease. I had thought I was doing well with my positive thinking and my eating organic, but my decline continued and I wondered if I would even make it to my 30 months. I had not repaired my leaky gut or built up my immune system to deal with the underlying genetic mutation. I still had a lot to learn and do. What I like about going to the support group is connecting with others and feeling good that others are inspired by me and my journey. What I do not like about going to support group is the non-organic snacks and food they serve.

# Amasai Saves My Life
## December 2012 | 30 months after diagnosis

Mid-November I did not have a good week. I couldn't catch my breath. While I was trying to sleep, I would stop breathing and my bi-pap alarm would go off over and over again. Then, I was having panic attacks. I asked people I knew to pray for me and send me good vibes and positive thoughts. The clinic doctor suggested I change my bi-pap settings, so I did that, too.

At the end of November, Leslie and I opened our Nature's Holiday Boutique. Featuring ornaments, package toppers, wreaths, floral arrangements, plant accessories and star wall hangings, we were open Thursdays and Fridays 11-7pm and Saturday 9-5pm for three weekends, selling all of our home, garden and holiday décor items we had worked hard to craft. It was a fun way to kick off the holidays, and we very much looked forward to seeing who would stop by for a little shopping.

December 12, 2012 was a fun date: 12-12-12. On my Facebook I encouraged all my family and friends to celebrate love and gratitude. "Begin preparing for your own personal transformation. Whatever that means to you," I wrote. "Look inside and let go of all your emotions and feelings that don't serve you. Let the new loving energy be amplified in your heart and share your love with all that you know." Living from a place of love is underrated. Truly, it is a powerful thing.

One of the biggest things I was grateful for in December

2012 was meeting a man named Jordan Rubin from the company Beyond Organic. Since the beginning of my ALS diagnosis I had been struggling with losing weight and Jordan Rubin changed that. He literally saved my life.

I had been invited to the event where he was speaking. He began his talk with quite a story of healing himself. I was amazed with the details of him using raw dairy. At the time, I couldn't process dairy of any kind. If I consumed any amount, I would pay for it with complete discomfort. This was when I was doing all these green smoothies. Well, in hindsight, learning that I was experiencing this thing called "leaky gut", all of the organic materials I was putting into these green smoothies were not getting absorbed. But back to dairy.

During his talk, Rubin said it was his cows that contributed to the healing of his body. I wanted to know what was so special about these cows. Well, they come from Africa. They are grass fed. They have never been exposed to chemicals or given antibiotics. A very successful vitamin formulator, Rubin had 9,000 acres in Missouri and Georgia, and his cows roamed the land producing a very healing dairy product.

Now, keep in mind that your average non-organic dairy product sold here in the United States is full of hormones, antibiotics and dangerous proteins from the feed given to the animals that produce the dairy products. And, pasteurization laws allow food processors to "flash" pasteurize their dairy at 165 degrees for as little as 10 minutes and call it safe. Rubin is standing there talking about his cows and his dairy products that he spends 12-15 hours pasteurizing at 105 degrees, because at 111 degrees or greater, the "good" microbes are killed off. What that means is that your typical dairy product does not have any probiotics.

Now, a couple years before I went to hear Rubin speak, Oprah had invited Dr. Oz Mehmet, author of "You: The Owner's Manual," onto The Oprah Show. While Dr. Oz was on Oprah, he mentioned the benefits of including probiotics in your diet. Most people didn't know what probiotics were. Probiotics help maintain a balance in your intestines as well as help you to digest food. Since Dr. Oz was on Oprah, most people have at least heard of probiotics. In 2012, while I had been consuming organic foods and probiotics, I had also been experiencing what I came to know as "leaky gut." Essentially, what I was consuming wasn't being absorbed.

After Rubin was done speaking, a friend of mine arranged for me to meet with him because of my special situation. I introduced myself as someone with ALS and told Mr. Rubin, "I rarely say that out loud or to myself."

"That's the way to think," he said to me, and he opened up the front cover of his book that he was signing and wrote down a recipe for me to immediately begin trying to help heal my leaky gut and get my intestines back in balance:

2 bottles of Beyond Organic Amasai (a kefir-like substance)
8 to 10 raw eggs from chickens who have a natural grass fed diet, no soy
2 cups organic blueberries
1 organic avocado
Organic vanilla extract to taste

This changed everything for me! I consumed this recipe every single day, and I began putting weight on. This is unheard of in ALS patients. In three months, I gained 20 pounds and I felt so much better. What I learned was that my "bad bugs" were not staying where they were meant to be - in my stomach and intestines until they exited my body - but were leaking into my bloodstream and then would end up in my brain causing anxiety and depression. I was not absorbing any of the good stuff from my food. This Beyond Organic Amasai healed my leaky gut and allowed for me to keep everything where it was meant to be, and absorb all of the good nutrients I was consuming. Within six months, I was able to consume dairy and just about anything I wanted. For me, that was anything organic and natural. I went by a favorite burger place I used to eat at all the time years ago, and I wouldn't even think of consuming their food now.

I order and consume 48 bottles of Beyond Organic Amasai each month and they ship it directly to my home using dry ice. I have done this since 2012 and believe it is the best probiotic available for me to consume. If through this book you become aware of nothing else that may benefit your health, this may be the best thing for you to know about.

# I'm Still Here
## January 2013 | 31 months into my diagnosis

Dr. John Lundgren has been my family doctor for more than 30 years. Every time he sees me he says I make his day. When I was first diagnosed with ALS, from his point of view, there was no hope. He literally thinks it's a miracle I'm still here. Many people do. July 7, 2010, I was given 18-30 months to live. January 7, 2013, marked 30 months. On that day I left a message for the neurologist who had given me that life-changing diagnosis to let him know I was still very much alive. Then, I packed my bags for some fun in Fort Myers, Florida.

Leslie and I planned to escape the Minnesota cold for five weeks. Our friend Tom Peters drove down with us in the van, and another friend, Bruce Johnson, met us in Florida after stopping to see his daughter. Leslie's son, Ryan, flew down for a week, and my son, Jeffrey, came down for two weeks. It was "Leslie and the boys" and we had a lot of laughs and great fun.

The condo we rented was about 15 minutes from the ocean and was very nice and large enough to accommodate all of us. There was a great pool and hot tub down in the general gathering area, and there were lots of people around who were retired. Most were from the Midwest or Canada and they, too, were excited to have a reprieve from the cold. Together we were all enjoying the hot sun on our skin during the day, and the warm weather in the evenings. This was when I first began the Beyond Organic Amasai so my weight and energy were still down and it was necessary each day for me to nap. I would get up and go do something in the morning, get back to nap, and then go have some more fun in the evening.

My favorite time was being near the ocean. Our excursions to the beach in Fort Myers, Sanibel and Captiva Island and our trip to Key West were really fun. Tom and Bruce were really great with figuring out a way to get me through the loose sand and onto the beach with long boards that they would set down and "leap-frog" one in front of the other until I was out where I wanted to be. When we reached our destination, the boards were lined up next to each other to form a square platform island on the sand. They topped it off with an umbrella to shade me.

We found the Fort Myers pier to be a hopping spot at night. There was a great band called High Tide that played once a week at the pier and we became regular groupies. Fort Myers beach is where we discovered and fell in love with the toy flash copters we later started to sell.

After five weeks of sun and Beyond Organic Amasai, a kefir containing more than 30 probiotics, I began putting on some weight and feeling a bit more hopeful, like maybe I'd make it to my 51st birthday.

When I was given my ALS diagnosis, the last thing I really wanted to do in that moment was examine and change my lifestyle. But for me, changing the way I viewed food was essential. I needed to be aware of every food, ingredient and drink I was putting into my body and what that food, ingredient or drink would do to my body. Before I had Lyme disease or any symptoms of ALS, my body, for the most part, felt fine. I really had no reason to put a lot of thought into what I was eating and drinking, much less examine how food could potentially be good or cause harm. Now, looking back, I can see all sorts of simple things that I was unaware of and was consuming that potentially could have played a part in where I ended up. For example, everything I ate that contained MSG, which is a neuro degenerative. By putting a great focus on my food and drinks I began to feel much better and have more energy which enabled me to live full days.

My legs were now too weak to walk in my walker more than a couple feet. I posted a note to my Facebook page asking for help with things like organic meals that could be dropped off or cooked at my home, lawn work, help organizing tax stuff, organizing the garage, hanging pictures, going through old files to throw, help selling items on Craigslist, help juicing, and companions to go on "walk-n-rolls" and other places with me.

Mid-April, the results from the collected specimen at the University of Minnesota were in and a genetic mutation was confirmed: C9orf72, a gene mutation in chromosome 9 located in my "junk" DNA, snip 72. This gene mutation is something I was born with. It's a set of instructions in my DNA used to build cells that affect my nervous system.

I look at a gene mutation like another toxin my body is exposed to. For 45 years my body was able to deal with it without any symptoms. After a series of events or triggers, my body was not able to deal with all these different things attacking my immune system, or as I see it, my cell by cell biology. This brings me back to the "bugs" in my body.

Thousands of molecular processes happen every second in your bodies, and each of us has good bugs and we have bad bugs. What's important is the balance between the good bugs and the bad bugs. The human body carries about 100 trillion microorganisms in the digestive tract. This is referred to as our gut flora. And these bugs in our gut are directly connected to bugs in our brain and central nervous system. What I have come to learn through all of these studies done on people who have ALS is that those who have done really well have gone to great lengths to detox the body and change the balance of good bugs to bad bugs. Toxins in the body or foreign chemicals cause an auto-immune response. Essentially the good guys are joining the team of the bad guys, and they don't even know it.

As Leslie and I began learning about epigenetics, which is how genes are turned on and off like light switches, we started learning that genes are meant to carry out certain biological tasks. Because the genetic mutation that I have is now found in 40% of all familial (in family) ALS patients, I believe within 4-5 years there will be a cure for this particular gene mutation. So I do not worry about my sons getting ALS.

ALS is so hard because there is no definitive test to confirm diagnosis. However, there are enough symptoms to narrow down as the patient declines. Each patient's situation and symptoms are different, so it's hard to have consistent guidelines of what to do to slow progression and live your fullest life. I do think ALS guidelines of what to eat and what to avoid would be beneficial. What's interesting is that with a genetic defect, even though you are born with it, you may or may not experience symptoms or issues in your lifetime.

The following day I had an appointment at the ALS clinic. I did not receive good news. My lung capacity was at 49% in December. Now, four months later it was at 37%. This was way lower than Leslie and I were anticipating.

In May, Dr. Dole's report on me showed very high levels of cadmium, gadolinium, lead, nickel and thallium. I had a lot of heavy metals in me. Where did they come from? I can't say for sure. What I do know is that they are used in manufacturing items similar to products produced at the ammunition plant just down from my Shoreview childhood home. I have come to wonder how that plant could have affected the ground water and impacted the people in the neighborhoods near it. Most likely I will never know for sure. To help rid my body of the heavy metals, I did 10 weeks of EDTA IV chelation therapy and glutathione.

I also did a DMPS challenge test to see how my liver and kidneys remove heavy metals. I found that I have a dangerous accumulation of iron in my liver. All other liver indicators were good. I was thankful for that. When I researched iron and ALS, it immediately came up with information that ALS patients have shown to have elevated iron in their organs including, possibly, the brain. I called my chelation doctor to see if that's something that would deplete my iron levels.

At the end of May 2013, we listed our travel trailer on Craigslist and sold it to some folks from Wisconsin. I was sad to see it go, but I knew I could no longer use it and Leslie and I would need the funds in the future.

# Be a Seeker
## June 2013 | 35 months after my diagnosis

*"In the end it's not the years in your life,
it's the life in your years."* – Abraham Lincoln

By June of 2013, I believed fixing my "leaky gut" altered the course of my ALS symptoms and the additional pounds I had put on breathed possibility into my life. But life as I knew it was still changing. I had been experiencing some central sleep apnea where my brain and the muscles I need to breathe at night were having some difficulties communicating so I would stop and start breathing several times while I was trying to sleep. When I would wake in the morning, I would feel as though I had never gone to bed. My sleep study results showed I had 16 minutes at 87% oxygen and 23 minutes at 88% oxygen. The very low oxygen levels (below 88%) meant I was in need of additional oxygen with my bi-pap mask at night. Low oxygen levels can result in motor neuron cell death and we didn't want that. No wonder I was feeling as if I hadn't slept when I would wake up in the morning. I was looking forward to seeing if the additional oxygen would help. With the added oxygen and the 10-week EDTA heavy metal chelation treatment, my central apnea stopped.

I had become too unsteady walking on my own and Leslie

didn't like it. When I climbed into bed for my afternoon nap, she took my walker away and shoved it into a closet. At that point the only thing I could do was surrender to the fact that the safest way for me to get around was to use my electric wheelchair full-time or have someone help me.

One day, I fell when trying to make a transfer from my bed to my electric wheelchair. Every day prior to that I would tell myself I'm strong, focus on transferring and do it. That morning, Leslie and I were talking and I got up on my feet using my walker, and in less than a second I dropped to the floor with my feet underneath me. It happened in a flash and I thought both my ankles were broken. Leslie pulled my feet out from under me and sat next to me on the floor. Both of us were kind of in shock. It just happened. We went to the doctor to get x-rays and thankfully nothing was broken. I just had swollen ankles and knees and a bruised ego. I knew that was the last time I'd be on my feet. Later we went to the garage and practiced using the Hoyer lift from the ALS loan closet to see how it would work to get me from my bed to my wheelchair, and from my wheelchair to the toilet. After 51 years of loyal service, I found myself grieving the loss of my legs. I told myself it would be okay. I told myself it would be fine. It would be different, but fine. While I told myself that, Leslie placed a call to a grief counselor and suggested we participate in a 9-week Renewing Life course at a place called Pathways.

Pathways is an organization that provides free of charge services, classes and support groups for patients and their caregivers challenged by a health crisis. They have this huge volunteer base of professionals to assist chronically and terminally ill patients. Having been in existence for more than 30 years, they have experience with processing the loss of life as an individual knows it. Accompanied by Leslie, I participated in the Renewing Life course which focuses on spiritual and emotional growth. Ultimately it helped to calm our fears about the intense emotions we go through when grieving yet still very much living. Believing this journey is a body, mind and spirit situation, we both found the course to be beneficial. We began examining what other things we needed to do.

For a while, with me dropping weight rapidly and beginning to lose the full use of my limbs, Leslie and I had a pretty hopeless feeling that I would not live very long. Our spending habits were a direct reaction to those feelings; we spent whatever money we had as if my world was going to end within weeks, because we felt like it could. By summer of 2013, financially, Leslie and I were limited.

We hung out at home and spent time outdoors enjoying the sunshine. Just feeling warm sun on my skin is so nice, and there is such an importance in our bodies getting a good amount of vitamin D, which comes from the sun.

In addition to soaking up the rays, we began trying to save what money we could in anticipation of wanting to go somewhere warmer during the most frigid days of Minnesota winter. I know I am a man who needs sunshine, and winter in Minnesota can really wear on me and impact my attitude and outlook on life especially now that my body is under such duress.

Mid-June we had a family gathering to celebrate my oldest son, Jeffrey, and his love for his wife, Grace. My mom and siblings gathered at the park and we had a potluck and shared stories and smiled a lot.

Later that month we read that Doug Koch had passed away. His wife Jackie was selling a track and lift so we called her. She told us about a supplement called ursodiol, which is synthetic bear bile created by a doctor at the University of Minnesota. This was interesting.

Have you ever wondered how a bear can hibernate for months and when it wakes up it can get up and go out foraging for food as if it had only laid down for a short little nap? If you and I were to lie down for months, when we woke up our bodies would barely be able to move. Well, bear bile is what enables a bear to hibernate, wake up and move around with ease. Bear bile is the molecule that protects a bear's cells while it is hibernating. In China, bear bile has been used for many years for medicinal purposes, and is a million dollar industry. You can find bear bile in teas and wines and drinks. Animal rights activists are furious because to get the bear bile, bears are put into tiny little cages and literally have tubes poked into their gallbladders to drain the bile for human use. To be able to get the benefits of bear bile without having to harm any bears is a big deal. This doctor at the University of Minnesota was having success using his synthetic bear bile, ursodiol, with ALS patients. So, I called him.

"Where are you in your progression?" he asked.

"I'm in a wheelchair," I said.

He sighed. He wished I had contacted him earlier. I wished that too.

I began ursodiol by taking one pill a day for the first week, two pills each day for the second week, all the way up to five pills each day the fifth week.

In late June, I spent the day having difficulty breathing and feeling as if I had cracked a rib. It was miserable. What made the day a little more enjoyable was a little yellow finch that kept coming to the window. He would come to the window and look in, look at the cross hanging on the wall, go to the next window, look in, go to the front window look in. *Maybe he's checking on me*, I thought to myself, *making sure I'm okay*.

Not feeling 100% is never fun, but having ALS, not feeling 100% caused me to begin thinking about death and dying. It was my biggest fear. I think that's pretty normal. I think no matter who you are when death creeps closer to your door, you start examining the life you are living and what you have left that you would like to do. I was thinking about that. I was looking online for stories of proof of heaven. I was thinking of my own personal "glimpse of heaven" experience and pondering "your work isn't done yet."

We spent Fourth of July at my mom's, but came home late Saturday, a day early. I wasn't feeling well and knew something was wrong. I was thinking it was pneumonia. When I woke up Sunday morning with a fever I knew something was up. By Sunday night Leslie took me to the hospital. It was real busy, but the people were great. The doctor there was insistent upon a chest x-ray and then an MRI to see what exactly was going on. I wasn't thrilled at the thought of an MRI. For a person who has difficulty breathing, lying flat on a table for any length of time is a great challenge. I got through it, and we learned that I had a blood clot in my lower right lung. To get there, a pulmonary embolism had to go through my heart. That discovery led to a load more of tests to make sure my heart didn't have more clots or other issues. After many tests and confirmation that my heart was clear of blockages, an ultrasound on my leg showed another blood clot behind my left knee. My dad's mother died of a blood clot. It came from a broken leg and went to her heart and killed her.

I was glad to hear my heart was fine. But I was put on a blood thinner because they make your red blood cells more slippery so they don't stick together and cause a clot. Being in a wheelchair and not moving or walking is a cause of blood clots. I also use an intranasal laser to separate my blood cells, and that's been proven to work too, but I took the doctor's advice and began the blood thinner. I'm sensitive to some medications, but luckily I have had no reaction to the blood thinner. I also came to learn that a side effect of ursodiol is blood clots, so it's possible the blood clot I had was a result of my taking the ursodiol. When I started taking the blood thinners I stopped taking the ursodiol and I continued my search for anything that would help me stop my ALS progression. I was determined. I had decided a life with Leslie was a life well worth living. July 9, 2013, I returned home from the hospital. The pain I thought was a rib issue was a pulmonary embolism (blood clot) in my lung.

I wasn't thrilled to have to be taking a blood thinner. I don't love any sort of pharmaceuticals. For some people Western medicine or "traditional medicine" works. They are happy with that. For some it does not. I have seen far too many people fill prescriptions and pop a pill to address symptoms without ever trying to figure out the root cause of the problem. Well, as individuals each of us has a choice, and some would say a responsibility, to explore other options. That is what I did. I opened my mind to the possibility there may be something else out there that will work for me. If I wasn't open to that, I may not be here today. Imagine.

I know change is difficult. It's uncomfortable and uncertain, and in most cases it takes a dramatic experience such as an accident, the death of a family member, or a life-threatening illness that causes a desire to change. For me, it was a diagnosis of ALS. Most likely I would not have made all of the changes I have without it. I would not be paying such close attention to my body and how I am nourishing it and how it is feeling. I would not be focusing on my spirit and how I am nourishing it and how it is feeling. I actually would be focusing on my mind and how I am nourishing it and how it is feeling because that is what I have done all my life. But I admit, physically, emotionally and spiritually, change is difficult. Sometimes it is necessary. What I know for sure is we never have as much time as we want, and Charles McPhee knew what he was talking about when he said healthy or not, time is an illusion.

Late July, I went for one of my ALS appointments. And actually, my mother and sister, Lynn, were there too. Dr. Gaurav Guliani, specializes in nerve and muscle diseases, like ALS and multiple sclerosis, and works at the University of Minnesota (U of M). The U of M is one of many labs throughout the world working on ways to change gene mutation. Dr. Guliani had been doing research there and was really interested in the C9orf72 theory gene mutation. Individuals from Finland accounted for 40% of familial ALS cases. With the highest concentration of familial C9orf72 cases being in Finland, and my heritage being Finnish and my having familial ALS, Dr. Guliani wanted to know if I would be interested in being tested for the C9orf72 gene mutation. He asked if I would be open to donating a skin biopsy to the University of Minnesota and suggested that I call the genetic counselor there to test me. The mission of their project is to find a way to silence the gene mutation and create from that gene mutation good, healthy stem cells. The take a sample, then clone the gene with my mutation and do research on the gene to hopefully find an antisense or away to stop the gene from misbehaving. I am hopeful this research is successful for future ALS patients. It's unlikely it will be successful in time for me.

## Genes and Methylation
Summer 2013 | 3 years after my diagnosis

In late summer, I posted an old photo of myself standing outside among the trees with my sons. I like to think that one day I will regain the use of my legs and be able to stand again. I know that's not what usually happens with ALS patients, but that's what I like to think. I suppose that dream helped to fuel my desire to participate in a new trial for my type of gene mutation that the University of Minnesota was doing. My appointment this day would be simple: a small skin biopsy would be taken from me to see if a new, unmutated neuro cell from my skin cell could be made. If it could, that new neuro cell would be injected into my spinal cord to help phase out the mutated cells in my body. I had my fingers crossed.

Just as everything was growing and changing within and around me, so was my love with Leslie. It was reaching new depths because I was learning to love myself in a different way. A good majority of human beings tend to live in the past. To live today for what today is, and love today who you are today, is a great accomplishment. Never before had I realized how greatly I am impacted by how I think. That little voice inside my head has a lot of power and what it says matters. I take time to check in with that voice and examine what it is saying now. I was who I was yesterday or the day before or the day before that, sure. That doesn't mean that's who I am today. If I look and see someone before me that I don't love, I tell myself to be brave and make some changes. Throughout my life I haven't always loved myself. I wasn't perfect. No one is. I try to remind myself of that and let go of that expectation. I try to look at the great things about me. I try to remind myself that I am an incredible man with this wonderful mind and I have a passion to share what I am learning with people. I look at that and I love that. I love me!

As someone who has been researching alternative therapies and supplements for years, I was surprised when I heard the word "methylation" from a friend at a support group at Pathways. The woman described that she has heard of a doctor named Amy Yasko who was reversing ALS symptoms by addressing the methylation issue. *Methylation issue?* I thought, W*hat's methylation?* As soon as I got home that day I began watching YouTube videos on methylation, the process of replacing a hydrogen atom with a methyl group.

All human beings have a methylation gene. Through YouTube videos I learned, be it genetic or epigenetic (environmentally caused), 33-50% of all Americans have the methylation gene turned off. I came across Dr. Kendal Stewart, a doctor known for his work in the autism community and his knowledge of methylation, and I learned that this is bad.

Methylation is the ability to process and eliminate toxins from our body. When your methylation genes are shut off – this is part of that epigenetic thing we need to learn more about –the body doesn't detox very well. Some people are polluting their body continually and they do fine. Others are polluting their body and they are doing awful, with more problems arising. Besides the fact that we should be doing everything we can to not pollute our bodies, the difference between these two categories of people is their methylation genes. Some bodies are just more efficient with getting rid of toxins. It's usually a family issue. I see that in my siblings, they are also holding on to heavy metals and are unable to capture and eliminate toxins. That includes all the pesticides, herbicides, food dyes, and what's in the air we breathe. The best way I have heard this illustrated is by describing your body as a fish tank – you have a broken filter in there and the water gets murkier and murkier. Sure you can put a few bottom feeders in there, but you still aren't eliminating anything. Doing Methyl B12 helps.

Dr. Stewart in his YouTube videos explained that methylation is responsible for all the exchanging of nutrients between the nervous system and our blood stream. This includes the nervous system's ability to store nutrients and detox the nervous system. Essentially, the nervous system, spinal cord, and brain are covered in fat. Methylation pathways are required to make the exchange of nutrients between this fat-based nervous system and the water-based blood system. Defects in the methylation lay the groundwork for further assault of environmental and infectious agents such as diabetes, cardiovascular disease, thyroid dysfunction, neurological inflammation, viral infections, depression, anxiety, fear, cancer, aging, schizophrenia, improper immune function, Downs syndrome, multiple sclerosis, ADD, ADHD, Huntington's disease, bipolar disorder, ALS, Parkinson's, Alzheimer's and autism. This methylation thing is a big deal! I began taking methylation supplements that Dr. Kendal Stewart designed, and I started encouraging the people around me who were having troubles to look at and learn about methylation.

## A Seed is Planted
### August 2013 | 37 months after my diagnosis

Time with family and friends is one of the great joys in my life. August 15, 2013, Leslie and I went to Flaherty's Arden Bowl to see some of our friends. They were having a food and school supply drive in honor of Jim Cunningham, their brother who had died. He would have been celebrating his 57th birthday that evening. The sun was out so we sat outside. There was a pretty good pile of donations for the local food shelf, and everyone was enjoying grabbing a bite to eat and talking a bit.

Heidi Schauer, Jim's oldest daughter, came over and said, "Kevin, do you have any tips for tummy troubles?"

Her aunt Colleen had told her I know a lot about foods. In recent years, Heidi had been suffering intense allergies. After doing allergy shots and being put on several pills a day, she began experiencing stomach pain. In May, she had decided to discontinue shots, and had taken herself off all her medications, but she was still having tummy troubles.

"Do you have something to write on?" I asked her, I did not want to waste energy having to repeat myself. She ran to get some paper and a pen. Returning with some small yellow post-it notes she said, "Okay, I'm ready."

"Coconut oil," I told her, "Add coconut oil into your diet."

"Coconut oil?" she repeated, writing it down.

"Yeah. Coconut oil is amazing. It's antibacterial, antifungal and antiviral."

Many people don't realize the abundance of health benefits coconut oil contains. Coconut oil is one of the very few things that can help an ALS person. It's a necessary oil for the brain. The brain is primarily fat so you need good fats and coconut oil is a good fat.

After suggesting she add coconut oil into her diet, I told her about Beyond Organic Amasai and methylation. Later that evening, Leslie and I found ourselves sitting at a table with Heidi chatting about health and friendship and God and the universe.

"Thanks for all the suggestions," she said to me.

"Yeah, no problem," I said, "I seem to know a lot about this stuff. My friends tell me I should write a book."

"You should!" she said, smiling. "Maybe I could help."

It was dark and past 9 o'clock, so Leslie and I hugged Heidi goodbye. A few days later, we received an email regarding our conversation. "If you want to write a book," she wrote, "I could help you do that."

Throughout my life I have wanted to share my experiences and what I am learning. But, there were so many times I was discounted or challenged by nay-sayers who thought differently than me. At some point I came to believe I needed some sort of credentials or PhD to talk about what I was discovering for myself. Well perhaps the letters of ALS are my credentials, because it seems that as people see me doing everything I can to slow my progression, they find great value in what I am thinking and experiencing and how I am dealing with life; how I am dealing with a terminal disease. Heidi offered to help me put my thoughts and experiences in a book, and that is how these pages came to be. She believed what I had learned and lived through was important. August 21, 2013, she came to my home for the first time. For four hours I told her stories and she typed while I talked. After day one, we had our first twelve pages. That was something to smile about, and on that day I needed a smile. That morning I had learned that my ALS friend, Paul, had passed away.

Heidi lives in a town about twenty minutes north of where I live. She is married, in her thirties and has two small children. At the time when we began this book, her son Tristan was three years old, her daughter, Destiny, six years old. After Destiny would board the bus for school, Heidi and Tristan would come to my home to help me write. I would tell stories and Heidi would type and ask questions. While we worked, Leslie would take Tristan to play. Some days they would sit in another room in the house. Other days they would walk down the street to the park. When possible, Heidi would arrange for a sitter and come alone. Without her passion for telling people's life stories, this book would not be what it is.

# Out of the Box
## September 2013 | 38 months after my diagnosis

In my constant search for healthy ways to slow the progression of my ALS symptoms, I had begun researching stem cells, and had found a YouTube video about Dr. Jason Williams who was a radiology doctor in Mississippi known for his "out of the box" treatments. He had a 30-minute video on ALS talking about the success stories he had seen and ways in which he was helping people. Dr. Williams had since moved from Mississippi to Bogota, Columbia where he was working for a biotech company named Neuralgene. When Leslie and I came across a press release for Neuralgene explaining their state of the art gene therapy development in treating ALS patients, I decided we needed to go to Bogota, Colombia. I requested more information and I got a YouCaring.com fundraising website set up. In a single week the generous dollars of friends, family and strangers came in and we raised more than $7,000. My devastating diagnosis of ALS suddenly had some hope.

In September, the ALS clinic in Bogota had their grand opening. Sitting in Minnesota in my living room, my hands continuing to cripple, Leslie outside in the garage sanding the cabinet doors from the kitchen and preparing them for paint, I dreamed of what this gene therapy could do and how it could change my life. I dreamed that I could one day, again, be out in the garage sanding and preparing cabinet doors for paint. I dreamed that I could one day again drive down the road to the grocery store. I dreamed that I could one day again walk through the woods and kick colored leaves and smell the bonfires of fall. I closed my eyes and dared to dream that the limits in my life I was now facing would fade as quickly as they had appeared. I dared to dream a miracle was possible.

For the most part I don't spend too much of my time or energy thinking about the things I can no longer do. Each morning I wake up and the day begins a little like a clip from the movie "50 First Dates." I wake up, think I will sit right up, swing my legs over the side of the bed, and begin walking to the bathroom. I open my eyes and think I will do that, because in my dreams I'm not ill. I don't wake up thinking I'm disabled. It takes a few minutes each morning for that reality to set in. It takes a few minutes each morning for the disappointment that I can't just get up and do the things I want to go do. But I don't dwell on it. I put my focus on thinking about what I can do. I can still use my arms partially. I can still swallow and speak. A year after ALS diagnosis my sister was no longer able to speak. I think about things like that and wonder what variables play a part in making my ALS experience so different from that of my own family members who have also had ALS. Pondering that makes me think I may be doing something right.

I was told two years ago I may want to consider a feeding tube. I didn't consider it. Even with some struggles regarding my swallowing, I did not want a feeding tube. Instead, I began paying more attention to always eating organic, eating more slowly and chewing completely. I paid attention to the possibility that there was still something that could be done to cure my ALS symptoms. I put my focus on my food.

The average person may not notice when a food is not actually serving their body well. I'm not sure I paid much attention to it before I had to either. But now, I notice. If I have a food I shouldn't, my mucus thickens and it makes swallowing more difficult. Take fast food for an example. That "grease" you feel sliding down your throat? It's not grease. It's your body's reaction to the food you are putting in it. Because I now have weaker muscles, it's hard for me to get rid of that mucus, so I've become ultra-aware of the foods that disagree with my body. I no longer eat white bread, bleached flour, cookies, pastries, pasta, or anything with refined sugar or high fructose corn syrup. To figure that out has taken time, but I'm making changes for the better. If you haven't already watched it, or you wonder why organic is worth the extra price, a one-hour video on the harmful effects of Roundup and GMOs can be found on YouTube. In my opinion, it's a video everyone should watch. It certainly explains the importance of what we are eating.

Monsanto is selling genetically modified seeds that are bug resistant, but you need to use their herbicides and pesticides. Is this safe for our food supply? My personal opinion is NO. Robyn O'Brien has a TedTalk video on YouTube regarding organic and GMO. You may want to watch it. Food is important, and I believe it is worth the time to do a little research of your own when it comes to the food you are putting into your body.

For someone with ALS (or any chronic illness or disease) aspartame is about the worst thing that can be put into the body. It is an excitotoxin used in foods and beverages that have zero calories. I cannot say enough how horrible diet soda is for a person. Synthetic growth hormones, soy, MSG – it is good to know what these things are and what they are doing in your body. They do have an impact and it isn't favorable for living your best, healthiest life. Even seaweed (which I discovered to be a problem with my Liquid Hope organic feeding tube formula) can have a negative impact because it is an excitotoxin.

Spiritually I was remaining optimistic. Physically, I wasn't feeling that great. I was noticing what I believed to be a major methylation detox. You may hear the word detox and think it's a place in a jail where you go to sober up from excess alcohol. I suppose that's one definition of it. Really, the word detox has become very much misunderstood. The best way to describe detoxing is to use this fish tank theory I heard, it's where you imagine your body as a fish tank. If you continually pour things into the fish tank without it having any sort of proper filtration system, the water in the fish tank gets murky and gross and becomes a thick sludge you can't see through or move. If you want to add a filter to the fish tank so the icky stuff can pass through, one way to do that is to purchase products that are "dirt" cheap, or should I say dirt and cheap. Ha! What I'm talking about is activated charcoal, zeolite and bentonite clay. These are all charged in a way that they attach to the impurities in our bodies and flush them out of our system or "detox" us. Sometimes when a person is detoxing they become very tired or even ill because the bad icky stuff that our bodies have become used to is being killed off. When we take the time to use the charcoal, bentonite clay or zeolite, I feel so much better. It really does make a difference.

My hope when I was feeling exhausted was that it meant some of the supplements and detox methods were working and my body was getting rid of some of the bad stuff it doesn't need. I was hopeful that detoxing would help with the many changes my body was experiencing.

Since being diagnosed with ALS, I've really began noticing the little things, like putting on my socks. Putting on my own socks is something I can no longer do, and because my legs are so thin, putting on my prescription compression socks takes a bit of talent. My prescription is stronger than others so getting the stockings on my feet is hard. Plus, I have super sensitive feet (especially to prickly things) that are always cold because I am sitting all the time and there is no circulation. My heated boots with rechargeable batteries helps with them always being cold. They may not sound that fantastic, but let me tell you, they are one of my greatest simple pleasures.

Leslie and I are always on the hunt for anything that will help with the latest obstacle. Another of Leslie's great finds was a soft bristle scrub brush we use for my feet because they are so sensitive. We do weekly magnesium foot soaks where we dissolve three cups of Epsom salt into lukewarm water and let my feet soak for at least 20 minutes. This is to help pull toxins from my body. Believe it or not, all human beings are toxic. We have toxins in the air we breathe, the food we eat, the clothes we wear. These toxins get into our bloodstream and affect how our bodies are functioning, living and surviving. Because my movement and circulation are so limited, any time I do these foot soaks (always in a metal pan, never plastic) layers and layers of skin shed from my feet like a skin shedding from a snake. That massive skin shedding is something I never experienced before ALS. The soft scrub brush helps to gently remove the layers of skin. Learning to rid my body of any toxins I can has become a big part of my world. So has creating an alkaline environment in my body versus an acidic one.

I read a really great book by a research scientist named Dr. Robert Young: "The pH Miracle." In this book, Dr. Young talks about the importance of us bathing ourselves in an alkaline environment instead of an acidic environment. In relation to cancer, our cells are duplicating themselves. Dr. Young has proven that when your body is acidic the cells will duplicate a little weaker every time you duplicate, where in an alkaline environment your cells will duplicate the same or a little stronger. Cancer cells, just like healthy cells, also keep dividing. In a weekend seminar, he presented strong evidence with Powerpoint slides and pictures, showing where cancer can't survive in a slightly alkaline environment of 7.3. Seven is neutral. 1 is extremely acidic, 13 extremely alkaline. Both are corrosive. Both can be used to clean a counter and it will kill bacteria.

Any coffee lovers? Coffee is acidic. It takes eight glasses of water to neutralize a single cup of coffee. It's beneficial to know that and to know if a food or drink you are about to consume is acidic or alkaline. Dr. Young explains that when a body is acidic, the organs will go into a self-preservation mode and try to neutralize the acid by encapsulating the acid and taking it away from the organs and storing it as fat and other things: calcium deposits, gallstones, and so on. To avoid putting on weight and dealing with such health issues, you want to look for the high alkaline food and drink items and consume those. To help my body as much as I can, that's what I try to do.

It's good to know, too, what vitamins your body needs. I try to get outside every chance I get and soak up vitamin D. Some days when it's warm and Heidi's here writing, we go outside and I race her son Tristan across the lawn. We all get a few smiles and laughs from that. Smiling and laughing is good for your body too.

## Facing the Realization
### September 2013 | 38 months after my diagnosis

By September 2013, there were a lot of changes happening. Leslie finally received a return phone call from Bobbi, the grief counselor at the Center for Grief, Loss and Transition in St. Paul whom she left a message four months ago. All this time we had been on the waiting list for new clients. I wasn't too interested in going to see a counselor when Leslie made the initial call, and I wasn't too interested in going now, but Leslie thought it was a good idea so we started seeing Bobbi.

I guess the hope was that we would feel a little better, because despite my goal each day to focus on the positive, dealing with ALS takes a lot out of a person, and the person who has the ALS is not the only person who experiences the diagnosis of ALS.

One of our biggest challenges was that everyone visiting me could see that I had gained weight and was looking good, and no one besides Leslie really knew about or understood the fear I was facing with my continued decline. I had gained 24 pounds, had cleaned up my digestive tract and gained flora, but my lung capacity had dropped fifteen points in the past twelve months. Currently at 35%, I could not have another 15 point drop or I would have to make the decision of going on a respirator or ventilator, which would mean a machine would be breathing for me. Once you go on such a machine, you never come off, and life requires around the clock care. One either gets an invasive tracheotomy (tube in the throat) or a non-invasive nasal assistance which is this tube on your face all the time. Neither appealed to me. Being on a vent was nothing I was going to consider unless I knew I could get off of it someday. Having a machine breathing for you is not the only life-changing aspect of having a ventilator. If I made the decision to get such a thing, I would need a licensed respiratory specialist at my home to suck stuff from my throat. To have that type of care can cost $300,000 a year. With my unwillingness to go on a vent, I would make the decision to continue to decline. With ALS, decline entails the loss of limbs and the rest of your body to the point you eventually get locked in and have the ability to move nothing other than your eyes. That, to me, is a very low level quality of life. That, to me, is not living.

I decided if I had another fifteen point drop I was going to call hospice. So, I had begun doing a lot of work on death and dying. But then, this new clinic in Bogota was opening and it was this huge ray of hope that made me rethink doing a vent because now there literally could be a way to get off of it. To grow new motor neurons takes months, but you can wake up stunned motor neurons and remove the substances that are blocking signals. My next lung capacity check was scheduled for October. I was hoping by then I would be going to see Dr. Williams. But what we hope for doesn't always work out the way we envision.

When I found the news release for the clinic Dr. Williams works at in Bogota, I felt like I was already walking at the edge of a cliff with this sense of urgency to do everything I could to stop the decline of my lung capacity. My lung capacity is essentially the only important thing. It didn't matter if I lost the use of my legs or my arms; if they got weak. But my diaphragm - that's what keeps me alive. I kept measuring myself to see if I'd had any strength losses. I had. I attributed it to stress and blood sugar. When Leslie and I would get real busy, we wouldn't get enough nutrients into me and that was a problem. Another problem that surfaced was that going to Bogota was no longer an option for me.

After speaking to Dr. Williams in more detail, I faced the realization that going to Bogota in the current condition I was in could be life-changing in a negative way. Despite the excitement of the news release and website, Dr. Williams' therapy did not currently offer the gene therapy/stem cell combination. In addition, Dr. Williams expressed his concern that other ALS patients had experienced difficulties with their lower lung capacity and the Bogota high altitude. I was already struggling with low lung capacity. The altitude, with a great deal of anxiety, was a consideration from the start, but with a chance at a one-time treatment that would provide a lifetime of benefit, the benefit outweighed the risk and the plan was that I would be on oxygen the entire trip. However, hearing that a few ALS patients struggled, and one ALS patient ended up on a ventilator in a Bogota hospital, I needed to choose another option.

Because the stem cell treatment that Dr. Williams is currently able to do (without the gene therapy portion) is also available here in the US with a greater reduction in risk and for less money, we devised a new plan to stabilize my symptoms: November 6th and 7th, 2013, I would receive stem cell treatment at the Stem Cell Rejuvenation Center in Phoenix, Arizona. While it was not the one time state-of-the-art treatment I had hoped for, this treatment did provide hope for increased strength and a plateau in my degenerative symptoms. The Stem Cell Rejuvenation Center opened in 2002, and while they are not ALS specific, they have provided treatment to many ALS patients. Once again, we were reminded of the ups and downs to dealing with a terminal illness, and we were thankful for this second option.

The procedure I was looking to have performed is much different than the surgical implantation of stem cells into the spinal fluid of ALS patients in the Phase I and Phase II clinical trials at the Mayo Clinic and a number of other sites. It is not covered by insurance, and would cost $7600. Without the donations we had recently received, I would not have been able to do this treatment. The generosity of others made applying and being accepted for treatment in Arizona possible immediately. I began planning for the trip, and continued my search for anything else that could possibly help slow or stop the progression of my ALS symptoms.

# On the Field
### October 2013 | 39 months after my diagnosis

While we were planning the trip to Arizona, I was emailed a link to the Keshe Foundation where I downloaded a paper that very much intrigued me. The research in this paper (and the Keshe energy unit it was talking about) addressed the cell suicide process and identified two triggers in every person that causes them to think they would be better off dead than alive. It suggested that one cause of ALS may be cell suicide. For me, I immediately thought of when I was a kid and my brother was in the war. My mom was fearful every day he wouldn't come home, and I was certain I would be drafted when I was 17, and that when I got drafted I would go off to die. For a five-year-old that's pretty intense.

Later on in the report, it talked about ALS individuals also experiencing a time in their life, typically 2-5 years before their ALS diagnosis, where they had some sort of trigger that made them feel like they'd like to take their own life. For me, that was the trust breach and fraud case I experienced where my identity was stolen and I lost everything and had to claim bankruptcy. That was a tough time. That was certainly an emotional trigger, and I did ponder whether or not I wanted to go on in this life. This idea of emotional triggers contributing to cell death was fascinating.

I searched for more information about the cell death pathway as a possible cause for ALS; this idea of cells in our bodies having a death wish, and ALS being a form of this death wish coming true.

Essentially, that is what this Keshe paper was saying. The Johns Hopkins University website and several others shared similar research about cell death pathways. The more I read, the more I could see a connection.

In late October, after watching a video about a man who used a Keshe energy field unit and went from being in a wheelchair to walking again, I skyped with Dr. Keshe in Belgium. My understanding was that the unit he created was a combination of magnetic and gravitational fields that can potentially stop this cell death pathway. I was hopeful his energy field unit could help me. Based on some tests he conducted over Skype, he gave me a 20% chance of walking again. The good news was he was willing to send one of his energy field units. The bad news was his suggested donation of $40,000. I was clear in telling him I was interested in the unit, but I would not be sending $40,000. What I did send was $3,500.

What I learned from Dr. Keshe is that his energy field unit is based on every cell in our bodies having this built-in suicide program. Normally, under your everyday "regular" circumstances, the cell's suicide program is kept under control. According to Keshe, your body naturally uses this suicidal cell death pathway, also known as apoptosis, to eliminate temporary cells that are no longer needed. There are studies by Packard scientists that show in individuals who have ALS, this process of temporary cell death occurred prematurely. It is believed that understanding cell death pathways is essential for future ALS research.

From what I understood Keshe also believes that our emotions and past experiences in life play a part in our cell death pathway. It makes sense. One of the people I first learned this from is a man named Bruce Lipton. He believes 99.5% of all cancer patients have unresolved issues which make up unforgiveness, resentment, guilt and shame. All those different emotions become part of and fuel someone's story that they embrace and live out. And everyone has a story. What can get in the way of us living our best stories is something called unhealthy beliefs. Brian Tracy, a famous speaker, addresses this. What he wants us to understand is that what we learn at age five or six we file away as being the absolute truth, the "gospel" if you will; the foundation for what we build upon. So, if at age five or six we learn in our own minds by who we are around and what we are exposed to, that we are brilliant and will become someone special, we build upon that. The flip side is, if we learn in our own minds that we are unlovable and will never amount to anything, we consciously or unconsciously build upon that. Our thoughts and the actions and words of others plays a big part in who we become and how our bodies thrive or don't thrive. All of us can acquire healthy or unhealthy beliefs. A book called "The Healing Codes" helped me to understand that, and has been transformative in my world.

I was also introduced to the work of Dr. Emoto who looked at the structure of water and studied how positive and negative energy impacts water and its ability to form crystals. Dr. Emoto discovered that positive sound vibrations create these beautiful crystals. Negative sound vibrations do not. If you were to write the word love onto a piece of tape and put the tape onto a glass of water, and for one week direct all the love you feel toward that glass of water, at the end of the week if you could freeze the water and examine it under a high-powered microscope, you would see these beautiful complex crystals. That glass of water would be much different than a glass of water that had say, the word hate taped to it. It's very interesting and proves the power of positive environments. After learning about Dr. Emoto, I wrote Love + Gratitude onto a piece of tape and taped it to the water glass that I drink out of. I know my body needs water, and I wanted it to get the best, most positive water possible.

With a terminal illness, and in life, you are either going to be the victim, or you are not. Even with genetic predisposition, I was doing everything I could to not be the victim. I believed that yes, I can influence the behavior of my genes and my thoughts. When I have a negative pattern that is cycling in my head, I contract every cell in my body and cells that contract don't work well optimally. I think part of the lesson I am learning with ALS is to let go and be free. Believe it or not, my days after ALS diagnosis are some of my happiest days of my life.

Within days of speaking to Dr. Keshe, I also spoke on the telephone with William Frey II, who is the director of the Alzheimer's clinic at Regions Hospital here in Minnesota. He shared with me some PubMed links and suggested I get melatonin and B1 to my central nervous system. Studies were showing oxidative stress to the brain is another one of the factors in causing problems for ALS patients.

That same week Leslie and I went to a flash mob at the mall in Roseville. I ran into a woman from church there and she told me I'm courageous for continuing to try to find a cure. There are causes for everything, and there is always something that we don't know that will reveal more of the mystery. The goal is to find that root cause of my ALS symptoms that will enable me to find the solution to the problem. Despite some difficult days, I remain hopeful that can be accomplished. Eckhart Tolle says in his book "The Power of Now" that what we all have is what we have right now. When I'm afraid or experiencing a time of uncertainty, I think of the power of right now.

Regarding the right here and right now, as I am experiencing changes and have things I can no longer do and items I can no longer use, I am repurposing. With my digestive system and what I am learning about my own personal body, I can no longer use my Norwalk juicer I had used when I did the Gerson Therapy. So, I sold it for $1,200. The juicer was amazing and valuable, but I could no longer use it so there was no purpose in hanging on to it. By selling it, I was able to move that asset to something that is better serving me. It's good from time to time to look around your home and your life and see what is working for you and what is not. If something is not working or being useful, consider doing what you can to change that.

## Positive Thinking, Positive Results
### October 2013 | 39 months after my diagnosis

As I prepared for our departure to Arizona, I was experiencing a bit of anxiety and I saw a post on Facebook that I thought was very fitting. It was an image that said:

> F.E.A.R.
> FORGET EVERYTHING AND RUN
> OR
> FACE EVERYTHING AND RISE

I strive to do the latter, and I can tell you firsthand, facing your fears is not easy. Fear and anxiety are sort of partners, and when a person's mind becomes overwhelmed as it often can, the overwhelmed mind retreats to fear and anxiety. By late October 2013, I was experiencing some anxiety about my upcoming trip to Arizona, and some fear over my lack of money. I was also seeing how caretaking was taking a toll on Leslie and impacting our love life. I was afraid that it would become too much and that, one day, I wasn't going to be provided for. I was struggling to trust that the many things in my life were all going to work out. I think a lot of people struggle with that. Many of us often talk about having faith, but to have faith and believe the really tough times are going to work out okay – that really takes something. But things do have a way of unfolding just as they should, and there is a peace that comes with believing that. I love Leslie. Leslie loves me. She is a strong, incredible woman capable of dealing with this disease and of walking down this path with me. My need to rely on her 24/7 can be trying, but our love for each other makes it worth it. Together, we can both enjoy this chapter. I watch uplifting messages on YouTube and read positive thoughts and prayers and tell myself there are gifts in these trials that we face.

Every four months I go to the Hennepin County ALS clinic. They have a team approach where they do a full neurological test, rate my arms and legs for strength, and check my range of motion. The lung capacity test is the big one. Four months ago in June, my lung capacity was 35%. Four months before that it was 37%. The slow decline is good, but I was hoping it hadn't declined any further. Interestingly enough, when I made my ALS appointment four months ago, I wondered if I would be here to go to it. Well, here I am. I set an intention for my lung capacity to be around 34%. Or better.

October 31, 2013, still experiencing difficulties swallowing, I went to my ALS appointment and discovered my lung capacity was up 3% to 38%. It was up. It had improved. I could not believe it! For me this was confirmation that putting my energy into doing everything I can to stop the toxins from entering my blood stream by fixing my gut, focusing on organic foods and drinks, and detoxing my body is key. Beyond Organic Amasai, which helped me to fix my gut, was the number one reason I gained twenty-four pounds, and I believe a big part of why my lung capacity was up. The lead neurologist at the ALS clinic was amazed.

"It looks like you have plateaued," she said, looking slightly astonished.

*Plateaued? Me? With ALS?* The thought of it was wild, but it certainly did look like something was happening. I couldn't wait to see how the stem cell treatment would help. After my appointment, Leslie and I went home and Leslie finished packing us for our trip to the stem cell clinic in Arizona. We were departing Minnesota in two days.

There were 1,680 miles between our home and the stem cell treatment center in Arizona. Our plan - along with our friend Bruce who was coming on the trip to help Leslie with driving and help me with some of my needs - was to take our time and drive approximately 450 miles each day. We would stay in hotels, and they didn't have to be handicapped rooms unless I wanted to take a real shower. My plan for many of the days was to simply transfer in the morning from my bed directly into the shower chair we brought along, and do my sponge bathing there. The only requirement our hotel room had was to make sure there was enough room alongside the bed for Leslie or Bruce to transfer me from my wheelchair into bed and vice versa. This worked well and didn't prove to be any sort of issue. We stayed in regular hotel rooms, and in the morning Bruce would leave the hotel room because the hotel room became my toilet room and shower.

We installed some speakers that were directed toward me in the back, because I'm kind of on my own back there. I would tip my chair back and listen to the music. Music is my life. I love all of the oldies; Santana, The Rolling Stones, The Beatles, Bread, Eric Clapton, Neil Young. I like soft, easy music for relaxing and meditating to. When I'm home, I rarely watch TV. I am always listening to music.

Our third night was spent in Gallop, New Mexico which had a higher elevation than I was used to. After a long day of driving, I was laboring a little more to breathe that night, and I was anxious to get on my bi-pap to ensure a good night's sleep and a rested body for the following day's drive. I slept well, and on day four we arrived in Phoenix, Arizona where we got settled into our hotel/resort.

I had thoughts of *Am I going to be okay?* but I set clear intentions of seeing myself successfully going through what I was feeling anxious about.

# Regeneration
## November 2013 | 40 months after my diagnosis

November 6, 2013, after a good night's rest in Phoenix, we arrived at the clinic at 11 a.m. for our first consultation with Dr. Ewald. Apparently during this first visit she usually talks to patients about the importance of their diet and the possibility for any necessary changes to ensure the best possible outcome for their stem cell treatment. However, my focus on eating organic and doing what I can to detox my body put me a step ahead of many of the patients; I didn't have to make those changes because I had already made them months, and in some cases years, ago. I was very impressed with the doctor and felt after meeting her that I was in very good hands. She was realistic in telling us she was optimistic about slowing my ALS progression, and that she has had some patients who see great results and some who do not. Because I had cleaned up my body I had a better chance of success in seeing results. Significant results could take a few months or even a year, and positive results would be little to no decline in muscle wasting or breathing.

November 7, 2013, was procedure day. We arrived at the clinic just before nine o'clock in the morning. My name was called and Leslie and I were immediately escorted back to one of the patient rooms where I was then transferred to a table. Instead of having to lie flat on my back, I was able to lie on my side which was easier for me to breathe. They drew blood from me, and injected lidocaine, a numbing agent, into my love handles. They pumped me all up with a saline solution that breaks up my fat cells a little bit, and left me to sit for an hour. When the hour was up, the doctor returned. Using a tool that was sort of like a rigid straw, she made two really small incisions, one on each of my sides which created a strange sensation. She then harvested approximately two cups of fat from my backside.

"This is beautiful fat," one nurse said. "It has a beautiful color and I think it's really going to work out well for you."

I smiled. Beautiful and fat are two words you do not usually hear together.

"Why the backside?" I asked.

"Well," the doctor said, "under the microscope, we have found that fat cells from the front side are stress fat, and the cells from the backside are much healthier."

The procedure was very invasive, which I am not a fan of, but I believed in the possibilities that would come with it.

The liposuctioned fat containing my stem cells was then put into vials and given to the on-site lab. By 11:15 a.m. the fat and stem cell harvesting portion of my procedure was done, and Leslie and I could leave. We needed to return at 2:30, so we went to the hotel where I could take a nap. While I was napping, the on-site lab at the clinic was separating out my stem cells from my fat. They also used the blood they drew earlier in the day to separate the growth factors from my blood and then mix them with the stem cell solution.

When we returned, the harvested stem cells that had been extracted and enhanced with growth factors taken from my blood and alternative sources were injected along my spine from my neck to my tailbone. They were not injected into my spinal cord, but along the spinal cord and into the tissues that surround it. The hope was that these stem cells would build blood vessels to bring more oxygen to my spinal cord. Many studies have shown that low oxygen levels in spinal cord fluid have resulted in motor neuron death. This low oxygen issue is why a hyperbaric chamber is used to stimulate and promote stem cell growth with higher oxygen (two or three atmosphere) to increase pressure and drive oxygen deep into the tissues and promote stem cell growth. I didn't see Dr. Steenblock, but his YouTube videos are available online. His 10-minute YouTube video on ALS is very good. Stem cells were also injected into key acupuncture points in my legs and arms.

An IV drip containing trace minerals, vitamins and mannitol was put into the top of my hand and used to help move the "stemmies" through my blood stream and through the blood-brain barrier. Mannitol is a substance known to open the blood-brain barrier.

As soon as the IV drip began, I was feeling weird, but I was receiving a substance I was not used to. We got three-quarters of the way through the IV bag and I was light headed. The doctor came in to put stem cells directly into my IV line (not through the bag). "Go slow, go slow," I told her, "I'm not feeling well."

Well, next thing I knew I opened my eyes and all these women were standing around me. Evidently I had passed out for a minute or two. The doctor had injected some of the stem cells directly into my vein. After I regained consciousness, I said, "Maybe we should finish this tomorrow."

"No, no," they told me, "We want to get these stem cells back into your body right away. They will be dead tomorrow, so waiting is not an option."

Inhaling stem cells helps increase their ability to reach and get through the blood-brain barrier, so next we did four intranasal infusions. A painless process, this essentially consisted of the nurse taking two syringes without the needles on, so only the plastic part, and counting 1-2-3, then shooting the stem cells up my nose while I breathed in deep to "snort" them. This was done two vials at a time into each nostril, twenty minutes apart.

The doctors said to envision all of these strong stem cells having little halos circling them. I did that and set an intention that the stem cells would reach the places where they were needed. We received some supplements and a packet of information, and some bandages for the two incisions in my backside. They said to call if we had any issues whatsoever, and by six o'clock, after a very long day, we were heading back to our hotel room. I couldn't wait to get some calories in me, and go to bed.

Since we didn't have to be back in Minnesota for any reason, and the weather was so nice in Phoenix, we started to look at possible options for staying a few more days in Arizona. As luck would have it, we were able to stay at a friend's parents' nice home at Apache Junction. For six days we soaked up the sun, sat by the pool, and enjoyed the view of the Superstition Mountains.

Day four of our extended trip brought with it a surprise when I woke up from my nap, got ready to eat and had a really hard time trying to swallow even water. *What in the world?* I tried and tried and when my swallowing was not getting any easier, I wondered what I was going to do. I wondered what was causing this.

Worried, I started to become very anxious and I did my best to focus on breathing and relaxing. The variables of what could have caused this ran through my mind, and the theory I came up with was that I had become very weak from the stem cell procedure and, some of the stem cells had possibly gone to detoxing heavy metals. When this happened, my liver and kidneys got overwhelmed and I became very weak. I think that is what happened. And that is another reason anyone considering stem cell treatment wants to be sure their body is cleaned out as much as possible before doing the stem cells, because the stem cells will go wherever they are needed. One doctor said they can be a very expensive antibiotic.

I was so weak my throat muscles were struggling to swallow. In that moment, Leslie, Bruce and I gave thought to going to an emergency room and scheduling a feeding tube procedure in Arizona. But, I was able to regain enough control of my swallowing to get some calories in me and get a good night's sleep. When I woke up the next day, I was feeling much better so we chose to stay a little while longer in the sunshine. We put a great deal of energy into relaxing and making sure we were getting the calories in me while I was strong and not tired. Bruce is a raw foods guy. He makes these great green smoothies, and he does a lot of things to make sure he gets the right fats into his body. He was huge help with my needed calories.

While some people worry about too much calorie intake, for me, calorie intake is a big deal in that I need to make sure I am getting *enough* calories into my body each day. With a lower lung capacity, I am using quite a bit of energy throughout the day just breathing. My goal for calorie intake each day is 2,000. Up until now, depending on the day and how tired I am, I've been doing fairly well at reaching that goal and swallowing my 2,000 calories on my own. However, this inability to swallow in Arizona caused me great alarm and it became clear I could wait no longer on a feeding tube. I don't have the reserves or the reserved process to use stored fat for energy, so the inability to fulfill my calorie intake needs would result in my body starting to use whatever muscle I do have for energy. That was in no way good.

With the prior difficulties of swallowing food and liquids in the past month, and this new scare in Arizona, we returned home to Minnesota and scheduled a feeding tube procedure to ensure when I am tired or struggling to swallow I will still be able to get the calories I need to stay strong. This would not mean I couldn't eat food like I always had, but it would mean if I was experiencing difficulties or too tired, I would have another option and options are good.

I made an announcement about my decision on my Facebook page and thanked everyone for their continued support during my ALS journey. Regarding my stem cell treatment, I wrote: This treatment has given me hope, strength and courage to keep going. Without your support I would not have had this opportunity. I can't thank you enough. I love you all!

We returned home to Minnesota the day before a yearly seminar at the Hennepin County ALS clinic. The seminar features Dr. Tiryaki, the lead neurologist at the ALS clinic. This year she was speaking about her recent experience at a national conference. Leslie and I decided to go and we were glad we did. The two hour talk on gene silencing provided some great information, and I was intrigued when Dr. Tiryaki said she was going to provide a little glimmer of hope that she has never been able to give before.

She talked about the C9orf72 gene mutation, which is what I have. There is now a Facebook page for it called the C9. There is a ton of money going into it. They see it as a way to halt 30-40% of the familial cases. Gene silencing. Essentially there is a set of instructions that are going out that don't match up with anything else, so they end up floating around and just turn into a toxic protein that attaches to the motor neuron and kills it.

This speech gave, hope for my siblings and my kids and other families with this. What's cool about this is that Dr. Timothy Miller states that once the gene is silenced, he believes the body has amazing abilities to heal. I do too. And if the body is able to heal, there is great hope for ALS people to restore some mobility, maybe even full mobility. With stem cells anything is possible to grow.

At this same seminar, I ran into an ALS guy. He was an engineer. He brought a study with him about melatonin from Germany. He said they are having incredible results with melatonin for mood and oxidative stress. Just before the trip I had gotten ahold of William Frey II, head of the Alzheimer's research department at Regions. He suggested collaborators in Germany were doing studies on melatonin. I've been taking melatonin every day. It prevents oxidative stress which is really going to help a lot with the energy of the body. When you have too many free radicals, the body gets overwhelmed. Melatonin is a tablet, and I'm consuming 3 mg a day. The guy at the ALS clinic is consuming 300 mg a day via suppository.

Most clinical trials you have to have a 50% lung capacity or greater. If you've ever done stem cells, you're excluded. So, I knew that there was no opportunity for me to be a part of this trial or any trial because of my lung capacity.

Thanksgiving was around the corner, and despite having to have a feeding tube put in, I was feeling thankful that in this vast galaxy of stars, dust and everything in between, I was doing what I could to not only exist, but to live and shine as brightly as possible. Comet ISON was scheduled to be going around the sun, and some experts said it could cause large solar flares that could ignite some big storms here on Earth. Storms had sort of become a part of my world. With storms a possibility in the forecast, I turned my focus to all that fills me with love and gratitude: my family, my friends, Leslie, my new stem cells, my passion to help others and myself, and God. I encourage you today and always to take a moment to look at all the blessings in your life and let yourself be filled with love and gratitude. Let it radiate off of you as brightly as a comet's solar flares.

Sometimes we need that glimpse of what another person's life is really like. Sometimes we need a reminder to be thankful for the journey we and others are on, and the work each of us is doing. December 3, 2013, I shared this video on my Facebook page https://www.youtube.com/watch?v=Fu86wIffib4 to give others a glimpse of my reality, and to remind them and myself to be thankful for the will to go on: loved ones who caretake, individuals who spend countless hours researching and seeking a cure.

December 6, 2013, I made the announcement on Facebook that I scheduled surgery to have a feeding tube placed directly into my stomach to ensure I would be able to get enough good calories into my body. This would help with the swallowing issues I sometimes faced, and also increase my energy.

On December 10, 2013, I had the procedure. I was nervous about the dyes in the sedatives they gave me prior to surgery. Dyes are so bad for our bodies, and they are in so much of what we eat and drink. I was really hoping I wouldn't have any sort of reaction to them, and I didn't. The procedure itself took about an hour. Since I couldn't eat before the procedure, my feeding tube couldn't be used until the following day, and I was too tired to chew and swallow my food, I went all day without eating and I was grumpy, tired, and experiencing more pain than I had hoped. I spent one night in the hospital, and the following day we tried my feeding tube out, and then I was able to go home.

At home, with our Vitamix blender Leslie was able to grind up just about anything for me to eat. But, the point of the feeding tube was for it to be used when I got tired and we knew I should get some calories in me. Otherwise, I ate like I always had. But, having the feeding tube to get the calories in quickly with little effort on my part was a good backup option. For those moments, I found online the only organic feeding tube formula. It is called Liquid Hope. This is a shelf stable, premixed, all organic superfood formula, which is fantastic, but it cost $8 for a 12 ounce pouch, so it's not cheap. The insurance company at that time would not pay for the organic feeding tube formula. They would pay for Ensure, a brand of readymade food containing high fructose corn syrup, canola oil, GMO products, and low-grade vitamins, pesticides/herbicides and phosphates that can be "poured down my tube." It's not the healthiest option for my body. To have the healthiest option I will have to find a way to pay for it myself. What a disappointment. (In 2015, however, insurance did begin covering the organic formula, which is fantastic.)

## Ups and Downs
### January 2014 | 42 months after my diagnosis

December 17, 2013, marked my four year anniversary with Leslie. To surprise my love and celebrate, I arranged for Heidi to bring over 48 beautiful red roses, a dozen for each year we've been blessed to spend together. Leslie and I spent the rest of the evening enjoying each other.

January 2014 did not start out the way I had hoped. I was experiencing a lot of phlegm and was feeling pretty tired. Then, January 2, 2014, while Leslie and I were up at the lodge in Sandstone, I was on my way to our van and was not wearing my seatbelt in my wheelchair. I slipped out and landed in a snowbank. Leslie wrapped her arms around me, got me onto a garbage bag, and dragged me across the yard back inside the lodge where she called a neighbor for help. Thankfully I wasn't hurt, but I was frustrated.

By the end of January we had begun using a baby monitor during my naps. That way when I woke up I could say "hello" and Leslie would hear me and come help me get up and transfer from the bed back into my wheelchair. The baby monitor helped so I didn't have to holler quite so loud.

We were able to get a 3 bedroom/3 bathroom condo on the beach for real cheap, so we decided that mid-month we would travel to Florida to spend six weeks soaking up the sunshine. In hopes of finding someone available to help with driving and making meals, I posted a note on my Facebook page to see who might be interested. We received a response from a friend. A woman she knew would be willing to travel with us, and after meeting her, we invited Cindy to come along. Five days before we were to leave, I got the flu. Getting the flu under any circumstances is not fun, but for me, with ALS, it's really not fun. I couldn't wait to feel better, load into the van and head for sunny Florida. We left January 24th.

From the start, Cindy and Leslie bonded. They had great conversation and laughed a lot and found in each other a much needed friend. They were kindred spirits. We packed the van full to the top with everything we thought we might need for six weeks in Florida, climbed in, buckled up and Cindy started out our 1,300 mile drive. We were moving at a steady pace, but being careful, because we saw all these cars in the ditches on the sides of the road. It was a nice, bright, sunny day, but the wind had picked up. Then, 20 minutes into our drive we hit black ice and our very packed van begins to slide and skate side to side on the road.

"Oh my Gaaaaawd!" Cindy screamed.

"Ah!" Leslie shouted.

*Shit!* I thought, sure another vehicle was going to smash into us and take off the back left corner of the van.

But we came safely to a stop, and everything got quiet. Then Cindy began driving down the road again. "Thank you for not yelling at me," she said, "We're going to pull over up here at the next little stop."

And after a brief moment, I said, "What, did ya shit your pants back there?" and we all began laughing.

For six hours, Cindy drove. Then it was Leslie's turn. In Indiana, there was a snowstorm. Leslie thought she was driving cautiously, but both Cindy and I told her to slow down. Next thing we knew, in the left lane, there was a minivan next to us that had spun around and was sliding backwards down the street. Leslie sped up to get past them.

The bad weather, icy roads, and my inability to drive was causing me to surrender to this situation and trust we would be okay. But I had to remind them: "Girls, you don't understand. We can't be like all these other cars and go in the ditch. To get us out of the ditch

– they probably wouldn't tow the van with me stuck in it. How would we get me out?" It was not an option. We had to think of the logistics of the situation, and we had to be careful.

The entire drive itself was an adventure, and at the end of each day we were happy to get to the hotel to rest. We traveled through Wisconsin into Illinois and on through Indiana. Somewhere in Arkansas the snow stopped and we no longer had to put our jackets on.

It took three days for us to get to Florida. We saw on the news that a cold front was coming and we were really glad to make it to our condo in Fort Walton Beach before it hit. The condo was beautiful. I rode my wheelchair right in and loved it immediately. Of course once we got settled, Cindy and Leslie ran out onto the beach. After the long drive, I took a nap.

Our first full day in Florida, I spent some time on the computer doing some research and Leslie and Cindy left to get some groceries. While they were gone, the fire alarm went off. We hadn't yet put the ramps up so I could come and go as I please, so I was in the condo with no way out. I could see there was no fire, but the noise was unbearable. I tried to call Leslie, but she didn't hear her phone. I was able to turn the thermostat down and hoped it would stop the smoke detector, but no luck. It blared its alarm for twenty minutes until Leslie and Cindy got home, and while I sat there with my ears hurting and anxiety setting in, in my mind I thought, *Well, that would be a way to go: burned alive. Seriously, what would I do if there was a fire and I was home alone and couldn't wheel myself out of the building? I'd be stuck. Inside. Engulfed in flames.* Leslie and Cindy walked in and they knew I was upset. They felt awful. I felt awful, too. I realized I could no longer be left alone, even for a little while. That was a hard realization. What we think happened is that the heat hadn't been turned on in a while, and when we turned it on, it burned some lint or something and caused the alarms to go off.

Good thing some groceries had been picked up because the next day we woke up and everything outside was covered in a coat of ice. Not what we were expecting in Florida. According to the locals it had been somewhere near 34 years since the last ice storm. The roads in and bridges from Okaloosa Island to Fort Walton Beach and Destin were closed. The people who owned the condo we were staying in had about a hundred movies, so there we were, iced in, watching "Bridesmaids" and learning Cindy loves the kitchen and is a natural with preparing good meals and helping out when someone is in need of something. We didn't ever have to ask her to help feed me while Leslie was doing something else. Cindy would just know and already be helping me before Leslie or I said a word. For the first time in many months, Leslie was able to sit and enjoy being with me, free from caregiving for me. Leslie was able to have a vacation.

Cindy gave this unexpected gift to my love: she revived her spirit and reminded her she is not alone in dealing with my ALS. I'm here, sure, but it's not the same as having a girlfriend right by your side each day to talk about the challenges. My ALS battle doesn't only take a toll on me. What I need, what we need to do to help slow my ALS progression – that becomes our priority and sometimes Leslie's needs get lost in that large demand. But in Florida, each day when I would lie down for my 3 o'clock nap, the ladies would begin their "happy hour" chatting about kids and life and paths, and Leslie was thrilled to have a girlfriend to share this experience.

To see her relaxing and enjoying herself was wonderful, but one day with all the fun, Leslie and Cindy forgot to turn on the baby monitor and they didn't hear me when I woke up from my nap. I couldn't move, and I couldn't yell any louder, so there I was, stuck in bed. I peed my pants. And with that experience, I developed a fear of what else could happen if I can't move or do something on my own and no one hears me. I know it's important to live out of love, not fear. I know it's important to embrace the blessings and gifts of every situation. But sometimes, the "what-ifs" take hold and they shake you.

Other days, we sat on our balcony watching the sunsets, watching the birds – mostly pelicans and seagulls. It was relaxing. We talked about the weather back in Minnesota. We were thankful to be where temperatures were in the 60s. Our condo at this resort was located in a little alcove where it faced the ocean. We were protected from the wind and able to get all the sun. We hung out there between the buildings quite a bit.

A week after we arrived, our friend Joe came to visit for a week and occupied the third bedroom in our condo, and his son,

Kyle, drove down from Georgia to stay with us, too. It was great. Joe and I would go for walks and talk, and we would spend time setting these good intentions; casting out into the universe these good vibes. Well, the day after he arrived, we walked past the front desk of our condo units and there was a huge box. In it was the Keshe unit I had been anxiously waiting for! I had ordered it back in November and it hadn't come, so I sent an email to Dr. Keshe explaining to him that I would be in Florida for six weeks. I had started to doubt the unit would ever arrive — which was hard because I had put a lot of hope into this Keshe system. But, here it was, all these pieces and parts in a big box with no instructions. None. There was basically a head rest that you lay back on the bed and lean into the head rest like a pillow, and then there's a banana shaped hard "pillow" from your nose back over your head to put your head in a field; there's magnets in both of these pieces. We put it together the best we could and scheduled to Skype with Dr. Keshe.

In the meantime, with Cindy, Joe and Kyle, we started exploring the areas around Okaloosa Island a little more. A lot of the people there have been coming for years to that same condo, so it was us and a lot of retirees. We met our next door neighbors, Leonard and Carolyn, from Wisconsin. They were hilarious, wonderful people. They were just real great fun, salt-of-the-earth types. It was Cindy who befriended them; it was Cindy who went for a walk each morning and talked to everyone. Leslie and I would sleep in until 9 or 10 every morning. Except the morning of Ryan and Meredith's birthday. That morning Leslie got up and went for a walk on the beach celebrating her twin son and daughter. Grown adults, Leslie's children are concerned about her future; they are concerned about when I am gone. I suppose Leslie gets concerned about that too, but my family and I have promised her she will be taken care of. Still, we've found ourselves on a difficult journey. In Florida we were thinking about that a bit and we were savoring our mornings together before we would go about our days trying to navigate what was to come.

Everyone's entertainment and my frustration for the moment was this Keshe unit. I couldn't sit in it. I couldn't put my body in it. I couldn't put my chest in it. We didn't know what to do with it. Finally, Joe and I got in front of the computer in Florida and spoke to Dr. Keshe in Belgium. He helped us with where to start.

"Begin with a half hour the first day," he told us, "Then an hour the next day."

He instructed me to slowly progress each day until I worked my way up to five hours a day lying with this metal helmet on my head. It sounded easy enough. When I was fitted for my helmet, Keshe didn't realize I had a bi-pap. My measurements should have been without it. I explained to Dr. Keshe that I was having some problems swallowing, and he said to take the green cushion off and make them two separate pieces then, so we did that. Through my computer camera Dr. Keshe looked at me and said, "I didn't realize you were this far along." Well, we ordered this Keshe unit in November. It was February, and things had changed.

Joe and I disconnected our Skype call and set up the Keshe unit the way we were told to, but Dr. Keshe didn't share much of a step-by-step procedure. So, I sent him some pictures of what we had done.

"No, no, no. Move it all the way back," he wrote back to us. I did what he said, and then I started with a half hour treatment February 10, 2015. While I lay there with my head in this field, Joe took a picture and I sent it along with a text to my sons and Heidi.

The next day, I did the Keshe energy field unit for an hour. The day after that, I did it for an hour and a half. But the fourth day, I woke up and didn't feel like myself at all. I was off. It's really hard to describe, but I didn't sleep and I felt like my body was just sort of buzzing like it was overstimulated. By that night I was feeling so off I didn't do the Keshe system that day or the next. I didn't drink my water from the special pitcher, and I had a major anxiety attack. I don't have those anymore, but here I was having one again. I used to have them, but after I fixed my gut and began focusing on my foods they simply faded away. I wondered if I was going to keep breathing. I was really having a tough time. I did finally relax and fall asleep, and when I woke up the next morning I was a little bit better, but still feeling very strange. I drank lots of water and believed it was going to pass.

I emailed Dr. Keshe to tell him I was not feeling well and ask what it could be. He didn't respond. I emailed him and asked, "Could this be heavy metals I'm detoxing from?"

He responded, "No, I don't think so."

*I don't think so? Give me something more, sir,* I thought. I had been waiting months for this machine which I was sure would help with my miracle. What else was I going to do? Feeling awful, I waited four or five days before I tried the Keshe unit again. This time I started with 15 minutes. The next day I used it for half an hour. Then it happened again where my body felt like it was buzzing and I had this sort of off feeling. So, I stopped using the unit again. Disappointed I asked myself, *What is going on?*

I rested for a few days and we got out a bit and hit a few hot spots in Destin. My favorite place was a bar right over the bridge from Fort Walton Beach to Destin. There's a group of shops and restaurants and there's a restaurant with an elevator to get up to a patio where there's a great view of the water and the birds and the dolphins. They had great Jamaican nachos and jerk chicken. And Cindy is a great cook and a baker. She got on the internet and found recipes for gluten free cookies and baked goods and she made this great banana bread.

Leslie spent some time by herself just reading books and reflecting, and it left her realizing she needed some balance with all the time she was spending with me and for me making sure my needs were met. We had been together 24/7 for quite some time now, and Leslie was realizing she was losing a little of herself. I imagine that happens with many caregivers. Leslie and I talk about living in the moment, but for Leslie, she was living in my moments. What I thought was working for us, was no longer working for Leslie, and I feared this woman I deeply loved would want to leave. In addition to loving her with my whole heart, at this stage with my ALS symptoms, I am completely dependent upon her. That's not an easy thing for a man. This one woman knows every single supplement I take, every single food I eat, and every single thing I drink. This one woman knows how to bathe me and change me and prepare me for my day with tenderness and love. This one woman knows what frustrates me and what fills me up and makes me smile. This one woman knows all of that, and no one else does.

About two weeks in, when Cindy flew home, Leslie realized she was in this beautiful place and now she would have to go once again from being lover to being friend and caregiver. She just hadn't ever thought she would be the caregiver for me. There was a time she was very resentful toward family members and my children for not stepping up to the plate. Then she struggled, asking herself, *What is there not to be content with where I am and what I am doing right now?* In Florida she was sitting on the beach watching this beautiful sunset thinking she should be thankful and this should be one of the blessings of her day, and it was, but she struggled with not wanting to take care of all my needs and just soak up the sun and the sand and do the things her soul needed to do. She wanted to spend her time loving me and being with me, but did not want to have to spend her time doing the constant daily chores of caring for me. It's the pottying and the pulling me out of bed and the not being able to take a shower herself in the morning. It's the getting supplements and the preparing meals. It's the need to be alert while I am napping and always be on, and the inability to take a moment for herself and just . . . be.

When Cindy left, Leslie struggled taking back that whole caregiver baton and again becoming the only one responsible for me. It wasn't so much the daily chores or the action stuff of having to be here at certain times and leave when I need to, it's that the schedule and the ALS demands never end. It never ends for me either. ALS and life decline are not for the weak of heart. They are not easy.

# Family
### February 2014 | 43 months after my diagnosis

Mid-February, my sisters Lynn and Lora coordinated their schedules so they could spend a long weekend with me in Florida. We enjoyed listening to the ocean, seeing the sunsets, smelling the salt in the air. We liked walking and rolling down the boardwalk. When we would hit the sand, we'd lower my wheelchair and bury my feet. I loved feeling the hot sand between my toes, but I was sad to not be able to walk the beach or jump in the water. The sand was so white it looked like snow, so for fun we took a picture and sent it to friends in Minnesota who were dealing with real snow. We went to the Gulfarium Marine Adventure Park and saw the whale and dolphin show. We went out to eat at and Lora was impressed I like to eat oysters. Mostly while my sisters were visiting, we sat and talked. Having the time to connect with one another was nice. I would have liked to share the experience with my boys, but they are on their own life paths, doing their own things.

## The Challenge of Change
### March 2014 | 43 months after my diagnosis

On March 6, 2014, my son Joey appeared on the new George Lopez show on FX. I was so proud to see all his hard work pay off and his dreams to be a successful actor come true. Three days later a dream of mine came true: using my cell phone, I took the first photograph I had taken myself in a very long time; my hands seemed to be working just a little better.

My sister Lora and brother-in-law Matt gave us the gift of one additional week together in Florida and we could not thank them enough. We were dreading going back to the winter snow and ice. One morning while in the shower, Leslie let the water and the details of my decline, and the idea of my death, rain down on her. She cried, and she emerged feeling like she needed to make some changes. As much as we didn't want to put any energy toward it, my body was whispering warnings to us that it was slowing down and will eventually die. Leslie was wondering what she will do without me and seeing a need for herself to go do some other things; to have some non-Kevin hours. She was feeling a need to go to work in order to prepare for when I am gone. After four years of not having a job outside our home and being available to go to appointments and travel when we could and needed to, Leslie was feeling a need to know she was still capable of making money, being self-sufficient and preparing for her own future. And she needed to know her needs, desires and dreams were important too. She was feeling like my caregiver and my friend, not my lover. She was feeling alone, because all of my time and energy was going toward finding a cure for my ALS symptoms and stopping my progression. I was doing what I could to stay alive, but in the process I was missing out on time *living* with Leslie.

The thing about me is that I'm the type of person who goes for what I want. I'm 100% all in, and in the moment, facing the situation I am facing, I am 100% trying to figure out how to stop the progression of my ALS symptoms, and if I could, reverse their impact. If I'm 100% focused on that, I'm clearly lacking the time and energy I am dedicating to Leslie. At the age of 50, not knowing how long I would be here or what it would be like when I was gone, she was fearing what she would do for a job. Would she still be employable at her age? Would she make a decent wage? Would people still find her skills valuable? She thought about things like that, and she thought about how she felt like she was living someone else's life and not her own. Our days were dictated by my needs and wants. There is a reality that a part of a person gets put on hold when they step up to be a caregiver for someone else. There is also a reality to the fact that there is a part of that same caregiving person that becomes richer with compassion and love through their act of caregiving. Caregiving, folks, takes something. It takes something special.

All of the thoughts, feelings and concerns Leslie was having was shaking up our world a little and the last thing she wanted to do while we were on a special vacation was break my heart by trying to talk about it, but the best thing she could do for herself and for me was to be honest. I wasn't the only person in this relationship with needs, desires and dreams. It wasn't easy to hear, but I appreciated Leslie's honesty. She wasn't telling me she didn't love me. She wasn't telling me she wanted to leave me. She was telling me she needed a change. Of course I had some fears. Any good relationship is a lot of work. This relationship has the added complications of ALS, a disease that kills bodies. I'm sure there have been a few relationship casualties as well. Would she eventually leave me? Did she deserve something better?

I quickly stopped those sorts of thoughts, because I knew Leslie loves me and I love Leslie, so we would find a way to make it all work. For now, in Florida, we were going to enjoy every hour of every day, the two of us, together. Leslie and I took a walk and roll along the boardwalk and just before the sun set, we captured the moment with a picture together. I posted it to my Facebook saying, "Even though we ain't got money, I'm so in love with you, Honey!" And it was true. I was and am deeply in love with Leslie.

After six weeks of sunshine and soaking up a lot of vitamin D, we loaded back in our van and began the 1358 miles back to Minnesota. We stopped in Louisville, Kentucky to visit with Leslie's stepmom, Lori, and her stepsister Dana and niece Montana. Going into hotels and taking the equipment in and out, napping in the van without my mask – there are so many things that are a challenge when traveling. To surrender to someone else driving you cross country, and to take on the responsibility of driving cross country with someone who has ALS, takes a lot of courage. I was proud of us. March 18th, shortly before my birthday, we arrived home to cold weather and a forecast of 2-6 inches of snow.

I continued using the Keshe energy unit hoping it would cure me. For the most part I felt an emotional change much more than a physical one. I had fewer negative thoughts that crept in. I felt a little less fatigued each day, too. That's kind of the big one. That fatigue each day is always an underlying issue. That had lifted just a bit, and I felt a little more light and free.

Part of this Keshe energy system is to put everything I drink into this blue insulated mug that creates a magnetic field. The magnetic field is using an ormus field. An ormus field is an energy field. The ormus field can change the spin of an electron and create some new energy. A simple example of an ormus field could be demonstrated if you got a tin cup, put a rare earth magnet on the bottom of it, then filled it with water and drank the water off the top center with a straw or the use of an eye dropper. Ormus is real exciting and has propelled this whole new research project.

In the 1970s, David Hudson who was an Arizona dirt farmer saw these sparks in the middle of his field when he was plowing. They would kind of come and go with nothing real consistent about them. Unable to figure it out, Hudson spent millions of his own money to find out the sparks in his field were ormus, a mineral that can also be found in our bodies. Ormus cannot be measured with typical measuring equipment, so Hudson's search went worldwide. Now there's about fifteen vendors online selling ormus products. With ALS, I may be able to plateau, but then how do I reverse and regrow? Ormus appears to be something worth looking into. These are literally minerals that we don't get anymore. People with low ormus are susceptible to EMFs or electromagnetic frequencies, which lower an individual's ability for their cells to work properly.

Dr. Keshe had said to me when we first Skyped, that by using these devices he created I should get more energy. My breathing takes a lot of energy. Initially at that time back in November, I could only hold my breath 19 seconds. He thought after I used his system a while I should be able to hold my breath for more than a minute. I'm not quite there, but I'm hopeful.

I continued to pay attention to and measure my strength. Even with the energy unit, I was a little weaker, in my core, than I had been the month before. Rolling over in bed was becoming more and more difficult.

March 30, 2014, I celebrated my 52$^{nd}$ birthday. To celebrate we went to watch live music at Moe's. At 52, what I know is that ALS has put me in a place where I spend a great deal of time thinking about what this life is all about and how I want to live out the rest of my days.

## The Brain/Gut Connection
April 2014 | 45 months after my diagnosis

By April, my research had me focusing on the brain/gut connection and how it impacts our neurological system. It is truly amazing once you start digging in how much of our human body complications are related to what we are eating and drinking. Allergies, ADD, Fibromyalgia – the list goes on and on, and each is impacted by what we are putting into our bodies, and how we are taking care of our bodies.

Some of the changes I have noticed since focusing on what is going into my body and how I am taking care of my body includes no depression. In my younger years, battling depression, I had tried many anti-depressants and nothing really worked. That was frustrating. What was worse was that some of the prescribed anti-depressants made my symptoms worse. What did help when I was struggling was spending time outdoors. Climbing the rocks, maneuvering the trails, breathing in the fresh air – that always made me feel better. I was right there in the moment and the rest of the world and all its problems were not even on my radar. I miss very badly being able to go hike and climb. On the bright side, this is the first year that I feel like I will get to travel again, perhaps to Florida next fall. In previous years, I wondered if I would even be here in the fall.

April 8, 2014, I began posting "Save the Date" notices to my Facebook because my good friends Mike and Judy Cunningham decided to host a Celebration of Life garden party at their home to acknowledge my being alive four years after ALS diagnosis. The party was something to look forward to.

Keshe suggested doing lymph massages, which I know are suggested when there is an anticipation of needing to cleanse the body of toxins that are being released. Well, they were releasing. I felt awful, but I was happy about it. It meant we were doing something right. It meant we were getting rid of some icky things from my body. I believe I had a major ammonia release. I say that because when my eyes would water or I would cry, those tears would sting very badly. When using the Keshe energy unit, I had more of those stinging, hurtful tears. I started looking for answers as to why the tears stung and why they were increasing, and I discovered that ammonia is released when you have a die off of Lyme bugs. I knew already that I had Lyme disease, so I searched online to see what I else I could do to help rid my body of ammonia. I found three amino acids and ordered them online: arginine, ornithine, citrulline. Those three amino acids are known to help complete the aura cycle and help detox ammonia. I began taking them the moment they arrived and within three days I had no more stinging tears, an issue I had experienced for years. Without the stinging tears, I've been able to read so much more and lately I've been reading "Jubbs Cell Rejuvenation: Colloidal Biology: A Symbiosis" by David Jubb, which focuses on protein and antioxidant synthesis that allows for our health to flourish.

Remember that Live Blood Analysis I had done? Well, that sort of relates to what Dr. Jubb is saying with not eating bananas. I didn't get Jubb's advice until I understood the science behind it; how red blood cells are formed and how the whole cell cycle works. Dr. Jubb used the live blood analysis to see if the food was a positive or a negative to the body. Typically, he would use 100 people from different nationalities to determine if a food was making a positive or negative impact.

Activated charcoal is something I continue to do. It helps to rid my body of mold, fungus, yeast and heavy metals by attaching itself to allow those things to pass safely through my body without reabsorption. It comes in pill form or a powder. I typically consume a teaspoon of activated charcoal in 8 oz. of water two days every week. Oftentimes it does turn my stool black, but I see it as a sign that it's working.

April 17, 2014, after not having been to the ALS clinic for five months, I received good news: my lung capacity had not changed. The doctors seem impressed, but didn't seem interested in sharing what I had done to stop the toxic overload in my body with anyone else. How would other people learn about this very important information? If they don't start looking at their body and the toxins going into it, people will die much earlier than they should. ALS people. People I know.

# Positively Fueling
## May 2014 | 46 months after my diagnosis

By May, I had made a difficult decision to stop gathering on a regular basis with my men's group. Life for everyone was going in different directions, and my experience was becoming one that did not fill me up. So, I needed to take a break in order to preserve the time and energy I was dedicating to those gatherings and put it into something else that would positively fuel me. But make no mistake, I continue to care about those friends and get together with them every once in a while.

I was looking at what exactly my body, mind and spirit need to survive and thrive. I had learned that if it had to, my body could survive several weeks without food. Without water it could survive 3-5 days. Without oxygen, my body can only survive 3-5 minutes. So it seems making sure my body is getting enough oxygen is very important.

Oxygen is the only natural substance that the FDA has as a drug. If you want to provide more oxygen to your body, you need a prescription to do so. My body is a body that has a disposition. My body doesn't do a good job of detoxifying. You know that person who can eat whatever they want, drink heavily all they want, and smoke cigars all their life and live to be a ripe old age? That's a person who has a body that can detox properly. What I was learning the value in getting more oxygen to the cells in my body. The best way to do this is to sit in a hyperbaric chamber. I got a prescription

# A LIFE AND LEGACY WITH ALS

to use one, and a good friend of mine ordered a wheelchair accessible hyperbaric chamber from a place that offers wheelchair accessible chambers. One of only two places to offer such a thing. My plan was 120-minute sessions each day for approximately 20 days. The only real side effect that I was anticipating was, because my body would be put under low pressure, having to clear my ears. I could do that. It was www.ALSwinner.com that really turned me on to this. There are four people who are really doing well. I was hopeful.

While I waited for the chamber to arrive, I called a gentleman named Dave Kane to talk to him about ormus. I got his telephone number off one of his YouTube videos. I see every telephone call as a possibility to learn something new and find another piece to the puzzle. This man had a plethora of information about ormus. I was happy to speak to him.

In the Keshe pitcher, ormus, the furthest of the fields, is located in the top middle. The magnets in that pitcher are around the bottom third of it and at the bottom. This is why I drink my liquids in that pitcher through a straw, so I can get them from that ormus field.

Dave's advice to me was to replenish my deficiency in ormus, and to lower my exposure to EMFs. If I could rate how important this information would have been to know five years ago – this would be way up there with heavy metal chelation and fixing my gut.

Jarisch–Herxheimer reaction is when the liver and kidneys are overloaded with toxins that have been flushed or dislodged in the body from something you have done and it overwhelms the liver and kidneys thus creates a low grade fever and a yucky feeling. When people experience this major kill off, they feel like crap and get discouraged, but after a week or two realize you feel a little better.

Many people are unaware of electromagnetic frequency (EMF) poisoning. Have you seen the YouTube video where a cell phone fries an egg? In the world we live in today, there are electromagnetic frequencies all around us and our bodies get overloaded.

I encourage people, when they are going to bed, to leave their cell phones somewhere else so they are not within 6 ft. of them while they are trying to rest their bodies. So, as you can imagine, I wasn't thrilled to have to have a bi-pap machine next to me when I was sleeping. In order to protect my body, Leslie and I did a little experiment where we took a large piece of cardboard and covered it in tinfoil. Our hope was to reflect the EMFs away from me so my body would not absorb them. We also began shutting off our Wi-Fi at night. Some people are not as affected by EMFs, but about 50% of the population has a sensitivity. I'm definitely one of the people who is sensitive. Remember when I was doing the live blood analysis and answered my cell phone? The analysis was greatly impacted proving my sensitivity. My feeling after we began reflecting my bi-pap EMFs and shutting down the Wi-Fi at night, was that I began sleeping much better. This helped to make the hours I was awake of better quality.

I was still struggling with losing strength in my core and not being able to untangle my blankets at night. It was maddening. Leslie had found some satin pajamas and that helped so the blankets didn't adhere to the pajama pants when I was trying to turn or flip over. To address my sore hips, the ALS Society sent a high-end air mattress that we placed over the top of my regular mattress. That helped a little, too. My left arm was weak enough that sometimes in the night I had to move it with my right. It didn't seem to bother me as much during the day.

When I am awake, I spend a lot of time in my house and one of the things I have come to love is watching the birds. My sister Annie once told me when I hear a bird sing, she is thinking of me. I miss her. I think about her when I see the birds gather in the feeder near the window. One will fly up and nestle in and all the other birds will move over a little bit and make room. They get along so well.

I saw a great post on Facebook. Pictured was a wheelchair and it said: I'm in a wheelchair. It's not who I am, it's just how I get around." That's how I feel some days. Yeah, I'm in a wheelchair, but I'm still Kevin.

By this time, Leslie and I were looking back on the chapters of our lives. Both of us had made a good living, had had good healthy jobs, had excelled and had become very much dependent upon our work for our self-esteem. Both Leslie and I had gone through trust issues surrounding money, struggling with relationships with our children and how to be a parent when you're an emotionally wounded adult and you have children wise beyond their ages. We found in each other someone who was a parent and understood and could empathize with the struggles. We found in each other someone who had the same drive to succeed, the same fun-loving spirit, the same passion to build a life together was appealing.

Over the years we as people and our lives together have grown and changed. A very large part of that is my ALS symptoms and progression. They impact me, they impact Leslie, they impact us.

Leslie was feeling a need to find a new job, a new outlet, a new spark that allows her a little time to take care of herself. I understand. But it's not easy for me. Even though we believed I would last longer than the 18-30 months I had been given at ALS diagnosis, we lived as though today was our last day. We traveled. We did things. But now, Leslie lives through me. She lives my schedule, her hours are dictated by my needs for the day. My care now requires more time than one person can do, so we're branching out and developing a new plan. We are exploring new options so Leslie can go back to living her life and be my lover and friend, and not so much my caregiver. We're seeking a new balance.

We laughed about the drastic change from our old Saturday nights: smelling essential oils and hanging out in a hyperbaric chamber. My, my how our "walk on the wild side" had changed. Still, it was exciting.

# Celebrating Life
## June 2014 | 47 months after my diagnosis

June 21, 2014 was a Saturday evening I won't soon forget. During summer solstice, my family and friends gathered at the home of Mike and Judy Cunningham in my honor to celebrate my life four years after my ALS diagnosis. The sun streaked through the yard and the laughter and stories shared could be heard as everyone meandered through the yard. James Schattauer strummed his guitar and sang songs, and Leslie and I stood in front of the crowd while my dear friend Tom Peter delivered my speech. I chose not to read it myself so I could conserve my energy and enjoy the evening as long as possible. I was charged up. I was feeling great. And it just about killed me. By the time I got into the van at Mike's and Leslie drove us home, I could not wait to get into the house and get my oxygen mask on. It was worth it. The entire night was touching and humbling. My only wish for the evening would have been to have my sons there.

The following Monday, Mike came over and cleaned up my entire yard mowing the grass, weed whipping and blowing all the clippings and leaves. It was a total transformation and I was thrilled. To top it all off, he volunteered to be the "yard guy" the rest of the year. What a gift. Then, our friends Rob and Cindy Hanzlik came over and completely transformed our garage. We could actually park two cars in there once they were done. I couldn't believe it.

The week after the Life Celebration, I was feeling completely bleh! My eyes weren't open as much and my energy was low. I just didn't feel well, and I was having negative thoughts and nightmares. One night I dreamed there were bears in my house that weren't very nice, and I couldn't escape them. Another night I dreamed I was going into a river and was not able to get out because of flooding. It was causing me to not sleep well, and what I determined was that I was having a bad detox from doing the hyperbaric chamber. For someone who knows their body like I do, I definitely notice these things.

In an attempt to help with my caregiving and give Leslie a little time to herself, I placed an ad on Craigslist for a roommate and caregiver. Leslie was planning to go away July 11th for a whole weekend which hadn't happened in a long time. I began meeting with people responding to my ad.

Not long ago my sister Lora, who lives in Washington D.C., went to an ALS conference. I asked her if she got anything out of the conference. What she told me was that she came to learn the placebo effect is more powerful than any drug anyone is doing. With the placebo effect, a person could be taking sugar or water or saline solution, but told they are taking some miracle cure, and because they believe it is a miracle cure, the sugar or water or saline solution starts to help them improve. This really speaks to the power of our minds. There's a book that has a collection of stories of people who had been misdiagnosed with cancer. What happens is that they manifest cancer because they believe they have it, but the biopsy shows they actually didn't have it when they were initially diagnosed. Our minds are these beautiful, incredible, amazing things. Perhaps my placebo effect was not listening to the doctors and not believing there was nothing I could do to slow this progression. Perhaps because I believed I would slow the progression, that itself slowed it. I don't know, but I do know your thoughts and what that voice in your head is saying matters.

I've done a lot of thinking about what I think and say and believe. I've put a lot of energy into fueling that whisper that anything is possible and I could survive ALS; that I could slow progression. It's been my constant belief that I could get better and that I could plateau at some point. That's why I've tried so many different modalities – that belief and hope of staying alive. Is what I am doing working? My voice is the same or better than it was a year ago. My dad and sister did not live with ALS long enough to compare where they were at four years after diagnosis.

I have noticed since using the hyperbaric chamber that the pain in my hips is gone. I've also noticed more strength with opening doors, using my cell phone, brushing my teeth. But it's a roller coaster. I'm up and I'm down. I'm drinking lots of liquid and doing charcoal and detox clay to help gather any microbes that have been immobilized. There can also be some risk in detoxing. Now we're immobilizing or dislodging deep seated metals that are buried in the bone. These can be reabsorbed in the body. That's why I do my regiment with charcoal zeolite clay, which has a very positive charge. The microbes are negatively charged so they attach to one another and can be carried out of the body safely. Detox is real telltale sign. When it gets real intense, it's necessary to take a break. Two weeks ago, I took a little break.

With Leslie looking for a job and me interviewing potential caregivers, I was experiencing a loss of security and a fear that I would be left and not cared for. Finally, I chose a roommate/caregiver who would spend four hours a day, four days a week, available to me. She would receive free rent. The ALS Association also provided a helper who came on Mondays for four hours to clean and do laundry. I had reached a point where I thought perhaps a group home would be a better option so I could be sure I had round the clock care, but Leslie and I got it figured out. I'm glad I will be staying in my home.

Our new roommate sounded perfect. She was an esthetician who told us she focused on living a healthy lifestyle that included organic foods. Most importantly she was available to stay with me while Leslie was gone for the weekend.

# Summer Alone
## July 2014 | 4 years after my diagnosis

July 7, 2014, was officially my four year anniversary of being diagnosed with ALS. I left a message for the neurologist that diagnosed me reminding him that I had been given a maximum of 18 to 30 months to live and I was still living. I told him there are some things people can do to live longer and slow their progression. I took a little time to acknowledge that it had been a tough-at-times but amazing four years. I posted to Facebook reminding my friends and family how thankful I am for their ongoing support and the part they play in my healing journey. Four years. That, to me, was pretty incredible.

Being without Leslie causes me some anxiety. Staying with and relying on someone else is stressful. The good part about it is having someone who can help with every little thing. The nicest thing I can hear is, "Is there anything I can get ya?"

Most recently I have been looking at the brain/gut connections and have been reading and watching YouTube videos about the heavy metals we collect in our bodies. Specifically, I have been learning what lead does to your brain. When I am feeling awful I use these EDTA drops to assist with heavy metal chelation and detoxify my body. I used them the other day and I noticed a change in how I was feeling.

The EDTA will chelate with all the heavy metals and my minerals and calcium, that's why it's used for cardiovascular

disease. EDTA is excellent for that because it removes calcium which builds up in the walls. With the hyperbaric chamber, the windfall of detox has been more than my body can handle. My kidneys have been sore. I had only a couple good days in a few weeks. And though I tried to be positive about everything I am experiencing, there were definitely days when I struggled with feeling like I was a burden and wondered why I
should go on. At one point I was doing some writing and I had these words come to me: What is your why? I sent a text to some friends, my sister, and my sons:

> 2:33 p.m., July 15:
> While writing a new poem yesterday these words came to me "I'm losing my why." Why do I want to go on, I asked? With so many things people can do and I have so few. I once again asked where is my why? If you can find it let me know."

Some people didn't respond to the text. Others sent hugs or prayers. My sister, Lynn, wrote a poem:

### Why?
### By Lynn Koll

I have a brother named Kevin,
He has seen a glimpse of heaven.
He's starting to ask "why?"
Why should I not just die?

He sees so many things
Others so easily do,
His hands and legs don't work
But his mind is there for you.

He looks at each new day
seeing beauty of outdoors,
If only he could move,

He'd love to do some chores.

He's here to shine the light
and give the world some hope,
He lives his life with courage,
and teaches ways to cope.

He's here to bring the change
the world so needs to see,
He's here to share God's love,
and true divinity.

In my searching for remedies online, I came across "A Miraculous Therapy for Grief and Loss" by Dr. Allan L. Botkin, Psy.D. It talks about EMDR eye movement desensitization and reprocessing suggesting that any image that is unpleasant to an individual, that individual can bring that displeasing image up in their mind as fully as they can, and having their eyes move back and forth, left to right looking at the image over and over, change how it occurs to them. To begin, that image may be an eight or a nine in terms of how badly it frustrates or angers the person. After ten minutes of looking at the image from the mind over and over again with their eyes closed, it might become a two or a one. Dr. Botkin was working with veterans who came back from Vietnam with traumatic images in their mind of people who had died. He also studied REM and what happens to the brain when you sleep. In working with these veterans, Dr. Botkin started having them pull up their horrible memories and do a series of eye movements while looking at those memories with their eyes closed. His patients, after doing these treatments, would come out of these traumatic memories with smiles and happy faces and they would state that the person who had passed would come to them in this open state of mind, and they now had peace. It's really quite a collection of incredible life-changing stories.

Trauma and negative experiences can really impact a person and their well-being. I was being reminded of that. My choice in a roommate/caregiver didn't work out. For good reason, Leslie and I didn't trust her. Instead of making our situation easier, it complicated it even more and we were faced with evicting our roommate and starting over. After sharing our home and our food and paying her to help care for me, I felt taken advantage of, and, I felt discouraged. Who will I find to help care for me?

I continued with the hyperbaric chamber knowing that if I could get these deep seated toxins out – that is what the chamber will do, it will purify every cell in my body. If I could do that – well, it would put me in a completely different situation. For now, feeling sort of icky as I detox these toxins, I have learned a great lesson in surrendering and feeling okay with whatever happens. It would be okay to go to sleep and not wake up.

Many days I have no energy. If I read seven pages that's doing pretty good and I'm exhausted and cannot read for a while. I'll have a conversation with someone and it will be great, but when it's done I am tired. I believe it's being caused by this detox or these metals that the hyperbaric chamber has dislodged floating around inside me. I don't have the energy or stamina I had before. I've just lost my zip.

There's been frustration. Dealing with me during my detox isn't that fun. I'm more irritable. Negative thoughts creep in more easily. I thought the chamber was going to be the Holy Grail. And right now, after our conversations in Florida, Leslie has other things she wants to be doing. I need an advocate for me. My mother tried to help by showing Leslie paperwork that she will get our house should anything happen to me. It's not signed yet, but the paperwork is done. I had hoped this would help with her need to feel like she has to have a job.

There's a new movie coming out that people are living longer with ALS. Eric from "Eric is Winning" was on there. He's weak, but he's on there. All these people, they are living a long time, but they are severely handicapped. This summer has been frustrating. I saw on Facebook my good friend Donny holding this big fish. It was a great picture, and I was happy for Donny, but I was sad for me. I sat there imaging what it was like for his brothers and friends to be there around him when he caught that fish, to be in the boat or even on the shore hooting and hollering with him as he reeled it in. About a week ago, around a bonfire, one of our friends said, "Your life really sucks." I guess I hadn't been thinking that way but since then I've been thinking about it.

I have been getting outside and going on some long rolls, but the fear of being stuck in my house for the duration of winter has begun. I wonder what it would be like to travel again, if that will still be a possibility.

I've been trying to focus on making sure I am getting more calories and I've been trying to make some notes about how I can get more independence. Foods can be out and at a level and location where I can get them myself. Coconut squares, grapes – I can lean over the table and get them out of a dog dish, I don't care. In the last couple weeks I have looked at group homes and assisted living places. The real problem for me are the meals. In my own little apartment, someone could cook for me and help me with things. But help could cost $5,000-$6,000 each month. I have friends, yes, but no one is doing the "poopy" stuff. I worry some days that Leslie will decide to leave and I'm just looking for something stable and secure. Leslie continues to tell me I don't have anything to worry about.

I've been thinking lately of that day of the four leaf clovers. How I said I would breathe God in every breath. I haven't done that lately. Let me do that now: *Jesus, thank you. I need your strength. I need your courage. Come to me if you can and show me something. I'm trying to shine my bright light on my fellow man. I don't know why me.*

During the finding of the four leaf clovers, it was clear to me that I was to shine my bright light, which I took to mean share these things that not everyone is seeing. I know my reputation is to be inspiration. I hear that from everybody. I think that's real, it's not a fake. Some days I struggle. This summer I'm struggling. I see friends out golfing and boating and walking the trails along the river. I miss that so badly. Either I'm going to get worse and check out of here or I'm going to get better. I believe the chamber is going to work. It's incredible. I believe in miracles. I don't know. I have one real optimistic side of me still, and the other is this negative side of detox. Do I regret doing the chamber? I don't know. At the moment, Leslie is on the job hunt and I feel a little alone in this world.

## Grieving Lives Lost
### August 2014 | 49 months after my diagnosis

In August 2014, ALS came knocking at the door. First I got stuck outside unable to get into the house or the van after the piston on my wheelchair broke. There I sat in the driveway with my legs stuck all the way up. I called for emergency handicap medical assistance. There is a 24 hour emergency number for Handi Medical Supply. They are the company that ordered and customized my wheelchair. We go in to see them once a year for a tune-up.

A few days later, Leslie and I talked to a hospice team from Fairview. To be sure we covered all bases, we reached out to family and friends to hear any experiences anyone else has had with working with hospice. I knew my energy had changed and I was feeling more out of breath, so we called the ALS clinic and got a last minute appointment. Four months ago my lung capacity was 37%. August 7, 2014, it was 33%. Had the neuroprotective qualities of the stem cells from my fall treatment worn off? Was it the toxins I had dislodged by using the hyperbaric oxygen therapy? Was it stress from having to kick out a roommate and being in a relationship transition? I didn't know. What I did know was that it was disappointing and a bit scary.

Leslie and I met with our counselor. We told her about the additional care we were trying to arrange. She thought that was a good idea. She thought Leslie needed to not be the sole caregiver and be able to have her intimacy with me separate from having to care for me. I hadn't really thought of how challenging that could be, to wear all of those hats. Of course, it's most convenient for us to have Leslie do the caretaking and not bring someone into our home. It's not always easy to have strangers coming into our home. But, for things like cooking, it's wonderful. Leslie loves to have someone else cook. Who doesn't? In many cases it's just easier for Leslie to do my personal care and relinquish the cooking and cleaning to other people. What we are realizing, though, is that she needs to take time for her health and well-being as well. She needs to go to the gym, or be able to stay in our house and go to a quiet corner and read a book.

August 15, 2014, we began this book project one year ago. In celebration, after Heidi donated the 221 pounds of food she had gathered from her annual food and school supply drive in honor of her father, she stopped over. For 7 hours we shared some stories and some laughs, and we did the ALS Ice Bucket Challenge, which was great fun.

This was the first year of the ALS Ice Bucket Challenge which was created to raise awareness about Amyotrophic Lateral Sclerosis, and also raise funds for research. How it works is an individual is filmed saying their name, who nominated them for the challenge, and in many cases who they were doing it in honor of if they did indeed know someone who has ALS, and then they would dump a bucket of ice water over their heads. They would then call out another individual for the challenge and that individual has 24 hours to take the challenge or donate to ALS research. In many cases people were taking the challenge *and* donating, which was wonderful. A lot of people donated to the ALS Association. Some people donated to other organizations or directly to people they know who have ALS. I knew a lot of people who did the ALS Ice Bucket Challenge in my honor. It made me smile each time. August 25, 2014, I shared on my Facebook the ALS Ice Bucket Challenge video of 26-year-old Anthony Carbajal, who is living with ALS and told his story with humor and heart wrench. It caught the world's attention and he appeared on the season premiere of Ellen giving thousands a glimpse a tiny idea of what this disease is like. It was incredible.

August 26, 2014, I was at the Moody Blues concert. It was a great night. The voices were great and the music was amazing. The following day on Facebook, I announced that we signed up for Fairview hospice. We were not looking at it as the end, but as a new adventure in life. I was looking forward to having more "family" and helpers for my journey.

Shortly after that my friend, Mike Fry, died. Life is so precious. He went in the hospital for one thing and never came out. He had a weakened immune system and very poor nutrition. I was really sad.

The reality was that both Leslie and I were grieving the lives we used to have. In some moments it was just like any situation when you are on one side of the fence wishing you could be on the other side. Leslie was realizing she didn't want to be caregiving. She wanted to be in love and spending time with her lover, not making sure my bi-pap mask is clean, my water is good, everything is hooked up right, and my pillows are comfortable and I can sleep. Our financial situation was another stressor. Frankly, I had outlived my life expectancy. Having no funds and needing Leslie to be home for caregiving was taking a toll. Plus, I kept searching for something that would slow my progression, some supplement or healing modality, and that was great, but that, too, came at a cost.

## Planning for the End
### September 2014 | 50 months after my diagnosis

In early September we were experiencing some stretching and changing with Leslie wondering what it is she is going to do when I am gone. Hospice helped with all of this. I find myself between acceptance and feeling like I'm giving up, and not giving up and continuing to seek a solution at all costs. I've done a lot of good things that I believe have given me extra time, but it hasn't been easy. Leslie is tired. I am tired. The uncertainty of it all becomes really hard to deal with. Meanwhile I'm getting some things done that need to be done. A green burial. I've decided on a place out in Inver Grove Heights. My eulogy. I've been writing some things down; some points and parts that have been coming to me, which I think are very humorous and funny. Hospice will help take all this responsibility of my care off of Leslie. I'm happy for that. I don't see them as the grim reaper coming for my final hours, but as a stress and pain management option to help maintain my quality of life, here to help me live out my last chapters.

I was told to get my Trilogy machine, a non-invasive ventilator, before I go into hospice. When you sign up for hospice care, you are no longer seeking life-extending treatments, instead focusing on symptom management and pain control. It is all about quality of life, not quantity.

Leslie and I enjoyed a day at the Minnesota State Fair and I had a custom t-shirt made of my Glimpse of Heaven. It's a white t-shirt with a staircase going up to an illuminated doorway. On the t-shirt it says, "I have seen the light." I love it.

At this time Heidi, who was helping me write this book, was gearing up for her daughter Destiny to go back to school. September 2, 2014, she had the best post on her Facebook explaining how Destiny's bedroom light was still on long after bedtime and she was so frustrated, but when she went to see why her daughter was still up, she found her drawing a picture of me in my wheelchair. With everyone talking about the ALS Ice Bucket Challenge, Destiny wanted to tell her teacher and her class that she knew someone with ALS. On her picture she wrote: "When I read I read at least 10-30 minutes. I started writing in 1-26-14 because my mom is helping someone named Kevin who has ALS a type of disease."

On the top of the picture Destiny drew some squares where she wanted to make a comic strip about me for show and tell. To know a 7-year-old wanted to share a little about me and how I have impacted her and her family, and how I have taught her what ALS is, is pretty cool. I wasn't expecting that. But I do hope that the way I live my life and what I share with others has a positive impact on them. I hope I leave something special behind when it is my time to go. I think I will. The lodge I built is part of that legacy I will leave behind. It's a place for people to get away from the city. It's close enough that it's easy for people to get away. Originally it was just a great get away when my boys were young, but now it's a really special place to a lot of people.

Leslie has applied for a job as sort of an outside consultant for Title I teachers and administrators. They need someone to coordinate their conferences twice a year. It's flexible and supposedly not stressful. She thinks it could be a good fit for her. Talk of her daughter's wedding has started. She's getting married September 19th. I'm not going to the wedding. That way Leslie can focus solely on her daughter during her special day, and she can stay as long as she wants without worries of having to get me home because I'm exhausted.

"My sister is coming a week earlier and we will start preparing for the wedding," she said.

"You'll be gone all week?" I asked.

"Yeah," she said.

"For the whole week? Where are you staying?" I asked.

"We haven't talked about that obviously," she said.

"You have to stay overnight in Plymouth because it's too far to drive or what?" I said.

"We'll talk about that later," she said.

"I didn't realize you'll be gone all week," I said.

"I'll be planning for Meredith's wedding. And yes," she said.

At least I have September 26th to look forward to when Leslie and I are going to see the Australian Pink Floyd show.

September 23, 2014, Leslie and I prepared for an estate sale. All remaining tools, old fishing tackle, building supplies, garage items, hunting clothes, books, electronics, art – you name it, we were selling it. I encouraged my family and friends to stop by, check it out and say hi.

A week after the estate sale, Leslie and I attended the Australian Pink Floyd show at the State Theatre. The music was great, but the bass was too intense for me to deal with. We tried moving up to the top floor, but left a half hour after we arrived.

The last two weeks of September 2014, we took a trip to Two Harbors where we met a woman named Karie Wright. Her specialty is homeostasis to reduce homeotoxicity. Karie has this homeopathic remedy and a few of these supplements I hadn't heard of before.

My body dealt with the misfolded proteins it had all of my life and functioned until I got Lyme disease. Then it became overloaded. Fifty percent of my siblings could get it, but don't. My sister Jan might have it now. She's five years older than I am. She told me the other day she is "brain free." Doctors were looking to see if she has a brain tumor, or possibly the dementia portion of ALS. It's very sad.

But back to Karie. She gave me some supplements and explained we're going to establish a nice, safe, but powerful detox method for me. She started me on three products by Energetics: Relax-Tone, a homeopathic that calms anxiety, Hypothalmapath to detox me and Lymphopath to carry the detoxed toxins out of my body. Water purification is key to success here so I am thankful I have my Kangen Water machine. We are also going to work on the gut with some lining support and cell support.

## Forgive and Let Go
October 2014 | 52 months after my diagnosis

We returned home and one night in early October my sister Lynn was over. We listened to this doctor on YouTube about mindset and having ALS and not identifying with the wheelchair. We talked a little about how to let go of emotions that run deep. When I say, "I've done my work" this is what I am referring to, this forgiveness and letting go that needs to happen. Learning to forgive is a big one because negative emotions go against everything in the body with that theory that Bruce Lipton instilled in me that positive vibrations, positive thoughts strengthen the body. I put myself in the position, and I think everyone should, where I thought: *If I was given a week to live, what do I need to do or say before I go?*

I thought about that and I did the things I need to do here. I made sure my boys know that I love them, and I made sure everyone knew I am okay with whatever happens so they should not worry about me or be sad. What I've realized is that in this vast wide world, we really are a simple grain of sand. We're here for a brief glimpse. Lynn and I talked a little about that and we had a great night together.

Mid-October 2014, my sister Lora was in town from Washington D.C. for work. We were able to go for a walk, visit, enjoy the fall colors, and have a family gathering with Mom and Lynn and Keith and others.

One night Lora and I sat at the kitchen table reminiscing

about our lives and our childhood, talking about the freedom we experienced. We kids of the 70s roamed the neighborhood playing outdoors until the glow of the evening called us in. Occasionally we'd hear our names called to come home, but for the most part we got to play and be kids. Lora talked about how she looked up to me, her big brother. She'd come watch me pole vault and ski jump. She liked my artwork. She saw me as a risk taker, and believed I was brilliant with my early business skills at such a young age.

She talked about the time she was five and I researched to find a good dog for us. Daisy, an English Sheep Dog, was wonderful. We had her until Lora was 19. Lora talked, too, about the less wonderful time when she was 12 and I crashed the motorized mini bike and knocked out her front tooth!

We talked about the early years when our family would go camping. When we had a trailer and we would go up to the Brule River and we would take over a few campsites and go tubing and exploring in the woods and have long campfires at night. Then at some point we started spending time at cabins. Every year we would take car trips. We drove to California, Florida, the Black Hills in South Dakota. Then I did my trip to California for a few weeks. We all did that. We went and stayed with Maureen Young, a cousin who lived in San Diego. She was married with two younger kids. We kind of helped with the kids. I was 15 when I went. I got to see the ocean. I was a good swimmer. Lynn, Lora and I were all good swimmers. We always went somewhere with a pool or water. People sometimes referred to us as fish.

"You were a terror with a slingshot," Lora said.

"Well, I had two younger sisters and was bored," I said.

She remembered that I did a really good Woody Woodpecker imitation, and that I would randomly blare the Three Dog Night song "Jeremiah Was A Bullfrog."

"Your drawings were always fantastic," she said.

She always remembers me being an artist. But I was so fixated on money, I chased after that.

I looked across the table and it was nice to see my sister, and it was nice to hear what she thinks about when she thinks of me. I told her about my recent trip to Two Harbors with Leslie and how we met a woman named Karie who talked to us about getting my body in flow. Every time I do some detox, I am retoxing too. I've started focusing on structured water. The way I'm structuring my water is that I'm using my laser to give the water an energy or a life force. The structured water and some supplements Karie gave us will provide a powerful, but gentle detox. It will take 2-3 months.

We talked about our sister Annie. "I remember already knowing," Lora said, "I knew at her 50th birthday party at her house that she was sick. It was her emotion about it and her hesitancy and her hyperawareness of the significance that there was something wrong. I felt like you were in a little bit of disbelief about that and you were convinced it was Lyme."

"Nine out of ten ALS patients in all these studies have got Lyme," I told her.

Knowing we had this predisposition in our family, I knew it was a good idea to minimize triggers: stress, trauma, significant medical. For anyone it's a really good idea in life is to just be trigger free.

"You loved to go to the state fair and do the cranes," Lora said.

I nodded my head yes.

"You were so good at it. Other people would put in their quarters and not get anything. You always got stuff," she remembered.

"You chose things to be good at and you mastered them. I love that you have passion for things. That's what I seek is people with passion and to hang out with people that care about something. Life is too short to be around flat people. Your continuous hope and ongoing search for livelihood and that vitality - that's what's different about your journey from other patients or other people in our family. Just keep on with it. You never give up. None of that is surprising given what I know of your life," she told me.

It was the acknowledgment and encouragement I needed at the moment. I could be full of rage or anger about this curse on my family. It would be totally reasonable for me to be stomping around saying it's not fair. But that's not who I am. I'm that guy who keeps on going. I'm that guy who despite difficult days continues seeking and researching and believing anything is possible.

Toward the end of the month, Leslie and I went with some

friends to Red Lantern Restaurant in White Bear Lake to celebrate Leslie's birthday. It was a fun night of conversation and some of the best sushi I have ever had.

I spent some time thinking about the past year. My swallowing is better than it was a year ago. I believe that to be because of stem cell treatment. An ALS person can stabilize, but improving is the big issue. That's why it's so important to be proactive and do everything you can to take care of your body and make changes as soon as you can. I believe in some way I can play a part in helping people with what they may want to seriously consider when they are first diagnosed with ALS. There's nothing out there. I'm learning recently that structured water and homeopathic is a big deal.

## Still Learning
### November 2014 | 53 months after my diagnosis

In November 2014, I learned about something called GcMAF. GcMAF is a human protein that is the director of your immune system. It appears for some reason that the production of GcMAF stops in your body and disease follows and this is the leading cause of cancer. This company in Europe has found a way to extract GcMAF protein out of live healthy blood and milk. I heard about it from the people who developed the movie Thrive, so I looked it up. I saw a video where they were only working with patients who had less than three months to live with terminal cancer and they would start using GcMAF and were experiencing as much as 40% tumor reduction in the first week.

I was grateful to have another Thanksgiving with Leslie. Last year I had wondered if it would be my last. We hosted Thanksgiving at our home.

November 29, 2014, my powerful wheelchair broke, so there I sat with no way to move. I called the emergency weekend repairman and he said he was on his way. Three hours later, I was still waiting. Those are some of the moments that are so difficult, when I am literally dependent upon others and stuck without them.

You know how you till the land and turn up the soil so you can plant new things and new things can grow? I feel like I've been doing a lot of that lately. I've been praying more. I've been openly sharing my gratitude and love more. I've been reflecting on what I do have. I still have horribly frustrating moments, but I breathe it out, and close my eyes and think about something good. I mediate. I listen to music. I think about things while I wait and wait for the repairman, and then I thank him for the work he does.

I am finding myself so thankful for the work others do. Now, with this hospice care team, Leslie is no longer the one solely responsible for my care. This team of professionals has given me the reigns, and they've given me possibilities and options. It's been good for both of us. It's changed my views on hospice care in that it isn't simply for someone who is dying tomorrow, though you do have to meet certain criteria to enter hospice. With a disease like ALS we deserve this special care. So do our loved ones.

The other night I had a dream that I won a marathon. It was a good dream.

# Dreaming
## December 2014 | 54 months after my diagnosis

Since spending a lot of time in my home, I have come to appreciate the windows. I love to watch the birds, and I get great entertainment out of the squirrels. In December, I watched this one pudgy little squirrel eat out of the bird feeder outside the window for four hours straight! I couldn't believe it. He looked like he was going to be sick. I'd be sick, too, if I did that.

This year, Laurie Littlefield included friends and family to bake and sell cookies for "Kookies for Kevin." It was the biggest Kookies for Kevin event she has done to date, and it was a special gift and so fun to see everyone who wanted to participate. The money raised was to help send Leslie and me to Florida if we wanted to go. A decision was made not to go. Leslie was glad. She had come to rely on the hospice care team and had developed a routine here. I, myself, would have liked to have gone to Florida one more time. But it was okay. We used the funds for other needs. Like each year in the past, Laurie told me she sold a few bags of cookies for next year. Laurie once said, "I do this for Kevin because he can't do so many things."

In late December, my son Joey was in town. He came to visit Leslie and me and we went to this fantastic butterfly exhibit at the Science Museum of Minnesota. It was so cool. I wheeled right into the very warm butterfly room and the butterflies fluttered around us and landed on us. I also realized how much I miss Joey and his exuberance for everything he does. He's created and is living his own life now.

December 29, 2014, Joey, Fin, Grace, Leslie and I celebrated Christmas. It was nice to be together. In the back of my mind I always wonder if it will be my last, and I don't know if my kids really get that.

In bed I can't easily roll over and my blankets get tangled. If I wake up, I just have to tell myself I am in the most comfortable position ever. I miss being able to just kick my leg out and tug my blanket up and roll over to get comfortable. I've also noticed when I wake up, my pillow and sheets are covered in my hair from my head. I'm losing my hair. I haven't used my feeding tube in days now. At the same time, I just had to turn up my bi-pap. My voice has changed especially when I get tired at the end of the day.

We've come to a new understanding of anxiety. Not good or bad, it's just a part of the present moment and living life and realizing you can't always maintain your anxiety. I nap and my back is sweating, soaking wet just from the energy I'm using to breathe. I am not a fan of prescription medicine, but I do believe at times there is a purpose for it. To help with some anxiety and difficulty breathing, through hospice I tried some Dilaudid also known to me as "dalala." I'm so sensitive I didn't like it, but Leslie saw that it did take the edge off and she felt that I was "the old Kevin" again. What it showed the both of us was that I'm experiencing more anxiety than I recognized.

Heidi came to work on the book and she was very concerned about her cracked tooth. Leslie has a cracked tooth too. Oddly enough they both had the same cracked tooth and they were both looking into getting them capped. Heidi was very worried about getting her tooth capped, especially since she has a silver amalgam filling in it already, so she was seeking my advice about the toxins released into the body during this procedure. "Can you explain to me what happens with this particular tooth when getting a cap?" she asked.

I suggested she consider taking some EDTA drops that day to help flush any toxins out. She felt so much better after talking to Leslie and me about her worries and concerns and hearing what we know about the body and toxins. That's a great part of sharing what I am learning, not that I am *the* expert, but just putting the information out there for people to consider and giving them sources to the experts. It can be a big help. Heidi did get her silver amalgam removed and she did get her tooth capped, and she thought perhaps her crumbling silver amalgam filling could have been adding to her health issues as tiny pieces of it unknowingly were swallowed before she was told it was cracked. Everything we put into our bodies has an impact. Dental work matters, too. Many studies have linked dental procedures to neurological and neuro degenerative issues. It's a good idea to look up any procedure you are going to have done and have an idea of how it can impact you. You can do this online at PubMed.

For our 2014 Christmas card we used the etching I did in high school of St. Francis. I found it a while ago and shared it on my Facebook, and a church asked if they could use it for a promotional poster. I let them. I loved that they liked it. I find it fun that something I created spoke to someone else.

I continue to dream of things in this life I would like to do. I'd like to obtain a handicap RV and do some more traveling. I'd like to design and have built a green house where I can grow organic food. I'd like to give back to all of the people who have helped me in my life, and all of the people who need someone to help them.

I watched a video about Dr. Timothy Miller at Washington University in St. Louis, Missouri. He's working on a new trial. The video did a wonderful job explaining the process of the C9orf72 genetic mutation. It is chromosome 9 that has the mutation and it lies in the junk DNA, in the snip of the chromosome known as 72, which researchers are just now discovering has a lot to do with the way our bodies get rid of toxins. The mutation makes a certain type of protein repeat itself too many times and this is what builds up on the motor neuron, thus making the neuron suffocate and no longer communicate with the muscles. This is why the muscles atrophy or waste away.

Dr. Miller is one of the head researchers right now in this piece with genetics, the mutations specific to ALS. His group has all the protocols for testing for a genetic mutation known as SOD1, a genetic mutation that many people have when they have familial

ALS. There is another percentage of familial ALS patients who have the C9orf72 mutation. So, they just received money from the ALS Association to continue all the phases of testing for finding the trigger to see if they can come up with an enzyme that would potentially halt or improve this gene, theoretically. You need to first go through some standardized protocols for testing. They are to have those in place from doing the SOD1 trials, so they are a likely candidate to find the antisense for the C9orf72 mutation. It will be at least a couple years out, and may be too late for me, but not for my family.

Leslie laughed one day when she came up the stairs and heard a familiar voice. She thought I was watching this C9 video again, but no, I was on the speakerphone with Dr. Miller. I had called him about three months ago and left him a message. He didn't call back. I called again and told him there was a possibility I may have some money to send his way. He called back. I asked him what was going on with the trials his team was doing. He explained they weren't even through the efficacy phase. I had been hoping they were further and I could maybe buy my way into the trial. If I could have, I would have found a way to get the money to do that.

The respiratory therapist has been over quite a bit lately. I've got my bi-pap turned up to nearly as high as it will go and I am still struggling with my breathing. They have advised me to use a Trilogy, which is a non-invasive ventilator. Where the bi-pap machine was more like an assist when I would decide to take a breath, the Trilogy is a machine that calculates for me and forces a breath. I haven't been using it because when I do I have horrible sleep. I guess it will take some getting used to.

Since I haven't been sleeping well I'm tired and I've had to use my feeding tube again, and with that I have been using the Liquid Hope organic feeding tube formula. We were using up to two bags a day and I was having a horrible time sleeping still. It seemed so odd to me. I wasn't associating it in any way with my organic formula, but one day I decided to look at the ingredients again. It was my only organic ready-made option, so I didn't give it too much more thought. The formula has seaweed in it. It's got wakame. I looked that up and for some people wakame is a sort of an excitotoxin. People with neurological issues are ultrasensitive to excitotoxins, even natural ones. I know I'm super sensitive, so, I stopped ordering Liquid Hope and returned to having more smoothies made in my Vitamixer. The next issue we faced was learning I was not getting enough greens and my blood got too thin. Leslie did get that job she applied for and started working as a convention facilitator. It will be a change. She's excited at the new opportunity. We're both thankful for our counselor, Bobbi, who we have come to trust, and who has helped us to work through many fears and obstacles to develop a plan and continue to love one another, and to realize our chapters of life together are ever-changing and there can be beauty after the most difficult of moments.

There's a lot of fun and joy and humor, but when I have a bad day, it's bad. Bobbi and our hospice care team are helping to make the bad days not so bad. They have re-ignited in Leslie and me a new faith and spirit and have given us a new strength that we may not have found if we hadn't been pushed to the brink with this disease. We've learned what hospice really means. Most people think of hospice as end of life, which it is. However, you can choose how you want to handle that. You can choose to have hospice come in and help manage care. I wish it was called manage care. It's unique and customized to each patient. I have time to ask questions and express to my nurse how I feel. I have time to express to my social worker how I am feeling and what I am going through. This is her specialty, families who are going through the transition of someone being very ill and possibly dying. She has wisdom and good suggestions to offer. This team is at my service and that has taken a huge emotional burden off Leslie's shoulders. It allows us to use my energy to do something fun with Leslie like when we went to the butterfly exhibit and all had such a good time.

At the end of December, my mom informed me that she was diagnosed with Stage IV lung cancer. She's a "snowbird" and lives in Apache Junction, AZ during the Minnesota winter months. During her trip to the hospital, she tripped, fell, and broke her femur just below her hip. January 2, 2015, she had a full hip replacement.

# Hope and Faith
## January 2015 | 55 months after my diagnosis

Actor Jim Carrey once said, "Hope is like walking through the fire and faith is like leaping over it." I have let go of my journey of hope and am now beginning my journey of faith. As I went to bed one night in early January, I told Leslie, "I'm okay if I die in my sleep." I needed her to know I felt okay if anything was to happen.

In late January, Heidi came over with Jessie DeCorsey, who is an incredible artist. Since the beginning of this book project, I had told Heidi I would love to have Jessie paint a portion of my story. We had a wonderful evening together and I told Jessie about my glimpse of heaven.

Four days later, I was very grumpy and I knew I was in need of detoxing my body. I took my first shot of GcMAF. Three days after that I spent the afternoon soaking my feet in a metal pan to pull the toxins from my body using Epsom salt.

My mouth gets extra dry from my Trilogy breathing machine and the long winter, and I'm experiencing a bit of cabin fever. Since December I have left the house only to go to a funeral and a few doctor appointments. I have had some good news though: my lung capacity has not changed in seven months. Essentially, I have plateaued. Guess I better wrap my mind around being here. Like this. Maybe I'll get kicked out of hospice? I hope not. They are a good group of people. Tuesdays and Thursdays one of the members comes and helps me shower, which I don't love, but it's nice for Leslie to get to take a shower all on her own and not worry about me. Patricia, the massage therapist is a total sweetie. And the music gal, she's got a beautiful voice. She helped me put one of my poems to music.

Our RN, Rick, visits every week from the hospice team. He comes and checks my blood. Ever since I had that pulmonary embolism, keeping my blood thin has been a priority. But not too thin. Rick has also been of great comfort assuring me I will not get kicked out of hospice. I was worried I might if I continued to do okay.

Luckily I am not someone who has a lot of pain. My hips are a little sore at night, but other than that I don't feel a lot of pain. I keep trying to focus on the positive; the joy in everything; what I can have and what I do have. I'm all about the music. Pandora channel is wonderful. Sound is great for anxiety.

## Beautiful Creations
### February 2015 | 56 months after my diagnosis

Mid-February I got the flu. Leslie took care of me, but then Leslie got the flu. Who was going to take care of her? She was. It wasn't fun. We were reminded again of the great importance in being still enough to listen to your body, and taking care of it by giving it rest and proper nutrition.

Late February, we were done with the flu and got out of the house with an adventure to the Como Park Conservatory. It was so nice. It was warm during these cold days of winter, and it was green and there were animals and beautiful flowers.

These incredible flowers that had bloomed will live out the duration of their life, and they most likely will not know the joy they brought to people simply by being these unique, beautiful creations. They will not know the positive impact they had such as bringing smiles and warmth to Minnesotans who were getting sick of winter. People are sometimes like flowers.

My Glimpse of Heaven left me with this passion for making patience, empathy and love a priority. I may not have done these things perfectly, but I did them to the best of my ability.

# Denial and Acceptance
## March 2015 | 57 months after my diagnosis

By March I began using a "Sip and Puff," a feature of the Trilogy machine which is mounted to my wheelchair so that when I feel the need, I can turn my head and take a puff of air. It waits for me to take a sip and it pushes a full breath of regular air into my lungs. This helps to save my energy. This also means that my diaphragm is weaker. I will have to decide how far I want to take the new technology to keep me breathing. The next step would be a tracheotomy and a ventilator.

In March, I received this really cool tie-dye t-shirt that was donated by Shy-Dye Ministries. Their mission is to put smiles on the faces of those with ALS. I loved my shirt, so they succeeded! It's great that there are organizations out there with the sole purpose of making people smile.

Leslie has been busy with her part-time job planning a conference for Minnesota Title 1 administrators and teachers. She really likes her work and I have noticed she is very happy lately. It's nice. While she's been doing that, I've been camped out at my computer researching. I'm not finding too many guru doctors who have anything new to share with me. On St. Patrick's Day, I had to share the great news I received from my friend, Jay, who was diagnosed with liver cancer last September. The doctors had found five tumors on and around Jay's liver. The largest tumor was 5.7 centimeters long and Jay was told there was nothing doctors could do; no treatments would help. I told Jay about a video I had found online about GcMAF and said it may be worth a try. The GcMAF was ordered, used, and the great news is that Jay's CT scan results yesterday showed an average 38% reduction in all tumors. He did nothing else but eat better and drink less. He and I are hopeful he will survive his terminal diagnosis! To celebrate that and St. Patrick's Day, I had a green salad with Brussel sprouts, cabbage and cilantro dressing, and a green smoothie for "Happy Hour."

March 24, 2015 was a sad day at our house. We found out our friend with ALS, David Eckholdt, passed away and then we heard that Bruce Kramer, who also had ALS, passed away on Monday. When someone who has been diagnosed with the same thing as you have dies, it hits home. It makes it really real and it's hard to stay in denial. You hope that they are at peace and you pray that they have faith, and you pray that they will see the light. Seeing anyone pass away is hard, but seeing people diagnosed with ALS after I was diagnosed pass away is really hard.

There's denial and acceptance and I guess I've lived with a little of both. Every time I imagine that this may be the last time I lay down in this bed, and that my kids and all family and close friends have been called and are stopping by to say goodbye, I have this knowingness that everything will be fine. The thought of saying goodbye to Leslie creates a big emotional hurt. I cry every time I even think about it just for a second, but again, I know everything will be fine. I think it's good to lay in your bed and practice this thought: If this was the last time you would lay down, are you okay with everything? Is there anything you have left undone in this world? If there are things that come to mind, make time to take care of them because none of us knows when it will be the last time. There is an amazing amount of healing that comes from having the conversations you need to have and taking care of the things you need to take care of.

Toward the end of March, I hired an EMF inspector from St. Paul to come and look at my house. Being that we are on a busy road and we've got a high tension powerline on our side of the street, our whole house is being affected by the electricity that runs through that line. In other words, there is a field that is created that is very measurable. The safest part of our property is the other side of the garage; the furthest from the front yard. Leslie's bed is better than my bed because it is further away from this major powerline. The EMF inspector, Kent, determined that in my bedroom, where I sleep on a steel bed and have a steel lift right over me, it was creating a very unsafe field to be sleeping in. Especially because sleep is when you do your regeneration and heal. So what Ken did is ground my steel bed through our own grounding rod right outside my bedroom wall. We also grounded the steel lift that is over my bed. The way Ken describes it, the steel things are antennas for EMFs; they act as conductors. So we were able to cut the EMF field from 5 gauss down to .05 gauss. It's not perfect, but a great improvement.

At the end of March, I received the painting Jessie DeCorsey was inspired to create of my Glimpse of Heaven. That painting appears on the cover of this book, and this book project has brought Jessie DeCorsey and Heidi Schauer together for another life-changing project. They refer to it as "a God thing" and say I have had a profound impact on their lives.

March 30, 2015, I made it. Fifty-three years old. This life has given me lots of opportunities. I have two amazing sons. I have traveled. I have learned to love myself. I have learned to forgive. I have experienced true love, found my faith, and have come to believe my body will die one day, but my spirit will live on. I have and continue to live an incredible life. I am grateful to still be here. I guess I still have work to do.

## UNFOLD
*by Kevin Pollari*

As the years go by I've seen it all unfold
I have learned so much of amazing things untold
So much fear in what is unknown
Finding your center can change your tone

From what I've seen, we lack in joy
Finding your truth is like finding a toy
Finding yourself, in the middle of a mess
Know it's your lesson, it's not a test

Finding the meaning in all that you do
Gives you the purpose, to see the day through
Trust that the lessons unfold, just as you asked
Resisting the flow makes it a task

I've asked God to show me the way
He said it will unfold just as you may
Connecting the dots gives you a spark
It has been confirmed, I'm right on the mark!

Unfold your heart like the wings of a butterfly
Sometimes it means saying goodbye
Unfold the months, season by season
Roll with the changes, no need to seek the reason

Lesson by lesson your life unfolds
Finding meaning brings you peace I'm told
Finding true love as long as it took
Gave me the strength to write this book

## August 10, 2015 | More than 5 years after diagnosis

I was inspired to write this as a song after church yesterday at Eagle Brook.

See the mighty eagle soar
It's you Jesus I adore
The love you give has no end
Messages of peace you always send
Putting you first is now how I live
Learning to live share and give
Like the mighty tree growing tall and wide
My faith in you assures you're by my side
Giving thanks to you Lord
My knowing of life ever after is restored
Watching the eagle soar
My faith lifts me off the floor
It's you Jesus I adore
I no longer fear no more

May you live fearlessly and love greatly.
—Kevin Pollari

## Kevin's "If I were diagnosed today" Top 11 List

ALS research is frustrating to watch. Not until we get down to the individual diagnosis of the actual cause of the motor neuron dying will there be a cure. Everyone is so different and ALS is a whole body disease. I believe it will be a cocktail of different medicines that will be the most promising. If I were newly diagnosed today I would:

1. Get tested for Lyme disease
    a. Testing by "regular doctor" may be inaccurate
    b. Seek alternative doctor to do electrodermal screening
    c. Test antigen with western blot test to help identify co-infections
2. Accept that I have this ALS diagnosis and be proactive in preparing for what may come
    a. Begin the process of getting my wheelchair
    b. Begin searching for a handicap van
    c. Make my home handicap accessible
3. Not accept the expiration date that is given, the 18-36 months
    a. Take each day as it comes
    b. Acknowledge that this is part of my path and gives my life purpose
4. Do what I can to be positive and live my healthiest, happiest life each day
    a. Surround myself with positive people
    b. Do not dwell on the negative
    c. Let my positivity be a testament to my strength and desire to live
5. Clean up my gut
    a. I CANNOT stress enough how important it is to clean up one's gut. Some call the gut the second brain. Beyond Organic Amasai had the proper probiotics to establish a balance between the good and the bad bugs needed in my body.
6. Put an emphasis on my diet to include eating organic
    a. Avoid all processed foods and anything with MSG, aspartame or soy

b. Eat fruit smoothies (more fruit, less greens), wild rice dishes, quinoa, chia seeds, nuts (no peanuts), Beyond Organic Amasai, wild caught salmon, sweet potatoes, squash, and coconut oil
   c. No soda or high fructose corn syrup
   d. Take glutathione, magnesium, high volume vitamin C
   e. Focus on alkaline foods
7. Drink properly charged water
   a. Spring water
   b. Structured water
8. Rid my body of toxins
   a. Heavy metal chelation
   b. Magnesium foot soaks
   c. Activated charcoal
   d. Bentonite clay
   e. Zeolite
   f. Remove amalgam fillings
   g. Make sure there is no aluminum in deodorant
   h. Use fluoride free toothpaste
9. Learn about and incorporate Young Living Essential oils
   a. Most oils are antibacterial, antifungal, antiviral, antiparasitic, anti-tumoral, anti-ulcer, anti-inflammatory and immune stimulating. Plus, smelling the oils brings these benefits right into the brain thus cleaning up the central nervous system.
10. Remove toxins from the home
    a. All cleaning products
11. Reduce electromagnetic frequencies
    a. Do not sleep near clock radio
    b. Limit cell phone use

## ACKNOWLEDGMENTS from Kevin

From the depths of my heart I thank every single soul who has been a part of my life's journey. To list them all would be a book in itself. First and foremost to God, Jesus, the saints and the guardian angels who have been there for me even when I was not present to their guidance.

Dick and Lois Pollari, my parents. They instilled the gift of freedom to explore this world uninhibited and encouraged my curiosity and sense of adventure. They rarely said "no" and that proved to be pivotal in my becoming a true seeker in this lifetime. My sons, Fin (Jeffery) and Joey who I love dearly; I am so proud of the men you have become. Leslie Hitchcock, my fiancé, for the love, sacrifices and adventure; for climbing mountains and conquering challenges. How lucky I am to love you and be loved by you. Andrea Pollari, my ex-wife, for 19 years of marriage, for the journey, the ups and downs, which I refer to as my lessons in life. To my brother and sisters (and their spouses), Keith, Annie, Jan, Lynn and Lora, who have shown me unconditional love. Phil Roche, who has always known how to add a little fun to the situation, have great conversation, and never leave a guy sittin' by himself. My Men's Group: Tom Peter, Bruce Johnson, Don Barret, James Schattauer and Adam Matz. What a gift it is for a guy to have some great friends who fearlessly share from the heart.

Over the years I have been blessed with a number of benefits to raise money. There have been so many people to thank and I have been overwhelmed and humbled by the generosity shown. The "Kevin Crusaders" led by Laura Flaherty and Tom Flaherty. My stem cell benefit led by Ginny Cone and accompanied by Bruce Johnson. Dennis and Laurie Littlefield for "Kookies for Kevin." To all of the friends who rallied when rallying was needed, donating time, energy, food and funds; and sent love and friendship with visits, phone calls, text, emails and Facebook. You have all been there to lift my spirits and I feel blessed.

A special shout out to my "Circle of Care," my Managed Care Team/Hospice from Fairview: Becky, for putting my words to music and creating four beautiful songs. Matt, for "making sense of it," Patricia with her gift of touch and massage, Rick for listening, understanding and patience, Angel for making me feel comfortable with my personal care needs and Sheila, who creates a safety net of care and guidance for me and Leslie. Sage Lewis, thank you for your present mind, inspiration and guidance. Bobbi Colby at the Center for Grief, Loss and Transition for your guidance along this path of change called dying. The Minnesota/ North Dakota/ South Dakota ALS Association for providing all the services you do! We have benefited greatly from the loan closet, the group meetings for ALS patients and caregivers, the Jack Norton Respite Care Program and so much more.

My buddy, John Roche, who passed away in 1995 from AIDS; I believe he came to me in my "Glimpse of Heaven" to show me what he wished he had known in his lifetime about the afterlife. By doing so he changed my life.

Heidi Schauer, for her energy, great gift of listening, ability to pull details out of me, and her perseverance to get this book done, which was no small feat. Thank you for creating such a tribute and legacy for me.

## ACKNOWLEDGMENTS from Heidi

I am enormously grateful to God for making me a witness to the lives of others, and for bringing into my life talented, strong, incredible people who bless me over and over again in unexpected ways. I am thankful to Kevin and Leslie for taking a chance on me, a woman they barely knew, inviting me to help tell Kevin's tale and being generous with what they shared. I am thankful for my father, Jim Cunningham, who taught me, by the life he lived, to put myself in another's shoes, come as I am, and give what I can. "Keep writing," he said. And I did. Thank you Kelly Cunningham for being my mom and for saying always, "Anything is possible." I believed you. Thank you Kelly Paradis, Andrea McArdle, Drew, Destiny and Tristan Schauer, Jerry and Faye Schauer, Pam Danielson Wolowski, Amber Cunningham, Colleen DeCorsey, Jessie and Trevor DeCorsey, Brian Bergman, Megan Cummings, Lynn Radmacher, Susan Schoon, The Forest Lake Writers Group, Dan Jurek, Don Sanda, Earl Weckman, George Martinson, my grandfather, who shared his stories of traveling the world while serving his country in the war, my grandmother, Bev Tarnowski, who spent most of her working days as a book editor, my grandfather, Uke Cunningham, who valued a good work ethic, my grandmother, Caroline Cunningham, who traveled the world through the adventures of books, the reading group who helped iron out the final details of this project, and, Rosella Dambowy, who in third grade told me she wanted a copy of the first book I publish. Without the encouragement, support and belief in me from these individuals, this book would not be in your hands. May we believe in ourselves, have faith, and dream BIG always (smile).

Kevin Pollari continues to live in Minnesota doing research to learn what he can to slow his ALS progression and maintain his energy for a better quality of life. His firsthand experience with seeing the light of God has given him a deep appreciation and a great strength for the lessons he has learned here on earth through this challenging disease known as ALS. He remains faithful that what he learns and shares has a positive impact on others and provides a greater hope for the next person diagnosed with ALS, though he continues to hope there won't be a next person diagnosed. Every day he is grateful for all that he has, and he believes living from the highest frequency of love, he will continue to change lives and his spirit will forever live on.

Heidi Schauer is a writer and photographer who believes every moment in life possesses a potential tale. She graduated in 1998 from Central Lakes College with a degree in photography. In 2001, she graduated with a Bachelor of Science degree from St. Cloud State University where she studied journalism, public relations and creative writing. Her adventurous spirit and outgoing personality have taken her from Anchorage, Alaska where she worked to promote the Special Olympic World Winter Games, to Uganda and Kaua'i working with Habitat for Humanity, across her state to meet individuals who make a difference. She lives in Minnesota with her family.

A LIFE AND LEGACY WITH ALS

"Don't judge each day by the harvest you reap
But by the seeds that you plant."

--Robert Louis Stevenson

For more information about the life and legacy of Kevin Pollari visit
**www.KevinsCrusade.com**